Marvin P. Osman, MD.

PLEASURE AND FRUSTRATION:

A Resynthesis of Clinical and Theoretical

Psychoanalysis

PLEASURE AND FRUSTRATION:

A Resynthesis of Clinical and Theoretical Psychoanalysis

LEON WALLACE, M.D.

International Universities Press, Inc.
New York   New York

Library of Congress Cataloging in Publication Data

Wallace, Leon.
  Pleasure and frustration.

  Bibliography: p.
  Includes index.
  1. Pleasure. 2. Frustration. 3. Psychoanalysis.
I. Title. [DNLM: 1. Psychoanalytic theory. WM 460
W191p]
BF515.W28   1984   150.19'5   84-3787
ISBN 0-8236-4161-9

Manufactured in the United States of America

To my patients, with whom I have had the pleasure of pursuing pathways to our mutual enlightenment.

CONTENTS

INTRODUCTION

Psychoanalysis is well established as a method of treatment and as a system of investigation of the mind. The development of a theory of the psychic apparatus based on psychoanalytic principles continues to be a central issue for psychoanalytic research. I believe that consistent and disciplined correlations between clinical observations and theoretical concepts will result in a better understanding of both aspects of psychoanalysis. In particular, further clarification is necessary of the roles of gratification and frustration in psychic development and in the therapeutic process.

It is axiomatic that every science begins with the development of a system of observation and passes through a stage in which basic variables are defined that are derived from the observations. The variables available to psychoanalysis, as in other sciences, consist of theoretical analogies. Robert Oppenheimer (1956), the nuclear physicist, justified the use of analogy in scientific research. "As an instrument of science," he wrote,

> . . . analogy is indeed an indispensable and inevitable tool for scientific progress. . . . I mean a special kind of similarity which is . . . the similarity of form . . . between two sets of structures . . . that are manifestly very different but have structural parallels. . . .
>
> It is a matter about which we could argue whether these structural elements are invented by us, or whether they are discovered in the world. [p. 129]

Theoretical concepts regarding a subject as complex as the "psychic apparatus" must be pieced together out of the jigsaw puzzle of clinical observation. In that sense, theory formation must begin as a synthetic process. This requires that relationships to clinical observation be clearly defined. Only when that task is reasonably accomplished can theories function effectively in an explanatory role and then be tested at other levels of conceptualization. The failure to understand this limitation is no doubt the cause of much of the abuse and distortion of psychoanalytic theory, especially that manifested by the proliferation of psychoanalytic schools.

Freud (1915c) provided the conceptual tools for a psychoanalytic theory of the mind in his metapsychological formulations. "It will not be unreasonable," he wrote, "to give a name to this whole way of regarding our subject matter, for it is the consummation of psychoanalytic research. I propose that when we have succeeded in describing a psychical process in the dynamic, topographical and economic aspects, we shall speak of it as a metapsychological presentation" (p. 181).

According to Freud, then, metapsychology is "the consummation of psychoanalytic research." This entails the view that metapsychology is, and must be, derived from psychoanalytic observation, not from speculations superimposed upon it. Regardless of Freud's own occasional propensity for philosophical speculation, a close, reciprocal relationship between metapsychological theory and clinical observation has contributed significantly to the development of psychoanalysis as a scientific discipline.

Glover (1947) appropriately described Freud's three metapsychological viewpoints as "basic mental concepts" and correlated them with the three fundamental qualities of mental activity observed during psychoanalytic treatment—impulse, memory, and mobility.

Impulses are reflected in the *dynamic* viewpoint. The existence of impulses, or psychological needs, is a necessary assumption for any psychological theory. The development in the individual of the inborn needs, or drives, from their infantile state to their adult manifestations, represents one of the most important contributions of psychoanalytic research. A dual instinctual drive theory fits well into the observation of the origins of neuroses as a result of conflict, that is, of opposing psychological forces.

During the evolution of the dynamic viewpoint Freud realized that some of the functions ascribed to the ego instincts (e.g., self-preservation) in his original formulation could be described more accurately as manifestations of narcissistic libido. He became alert to the greater significance of aggression at about the same time. The replacement of the concept of ego-instinctual drives by the aggressive drive, so crucial to the clinical development of psychoanalysis, took place within the theoretical framework provided by Freud's metapsychology.

Likewise, the evolution of the *structural* theory from the topographic viewpoint was stimulated by an integration of clinical observations into existing metapsychological theory. Neurotic conflict was originally represented as opposing forces: consciousness—acting at the behest of the ego instincts—versus the unconscious. Clinical observations that the patient's resistances are often unconscious forced Freud to revise his theoretical framework. Neurotic conflict then came to be represented as the forces of ego and superego against the id. The ego reflected the influence of childhood interactions with the environment and demonstrated the influence of *memory* on adult patterns of regulation. This was a much more sophisticated and flexible concept that derived from the integration of theory and observation, and it opened the field of clinical research to expanded areas of observation and reconstruction.

Rapaport and Gill (1959) suggested two additional points of view that I believe should be subsumed under the structural viewpoint. Their "genetic" viewpoint reflects the influence of memory on the psychic apparatus and, I think, does not warrant the establishment of another theoretical concept. Their "adaptive" viewpoint seems to confuse the psychic apparatus itself with its interaction with the external world. I think that its intrapsychic aspect is also implied in the structural viewpoint.

The *mobility* of impulses is derived from clinical observations of the associative process and transference phenomena (see, e.g., Loewald, 1960). These phenomena are integrated with the theoretical concept of psychic discharge, a concept of psychic energy, and are described by the *economic* viewpoint. During his investigation of dreams, Freud (1900) suggested that the psychic apparatus operates primarily in such a manner as to avoid an accumulation of excitations and to discharge such accumulations as soon as possible—the pleasure principle. The phenomena of pleasure and unpleasure, the foundations of human experience, were considered to be associated with the accumulation and discharge of excitations, although with significant exceptions.

Freud apparently alternated between his clinical and theoretical discoveries and left behind a number of important unresolved theoretical issues. To acknowledge that both his clinical and theoretical formulations were incomplete does not diminish their importance. Rather, it expresses an appreciation of the magnitude of his work. Freud was fully aware of the loose ends in his work and made no pretense as to the completeness of his formulations. In particular, the fundamental concepts related to the roles of pleasure and unpleasure in the psychic apparatus were never satisfactorily resolved and integrated into the metapsychological model of the psychic apparatus.

This was a consequence, I believe, of Freud's questionable assumption that psychic development is initiated by frustration. Also, the primary role of aggression as an instinctual drive was developed late, and its relationship to libido was not clearly formulated, especially in regard to ego development. Theoretical concepts related to the role of aggression in the phenomena of "identification" and "sublimation" have remained confused, even as the parallel clinical concepts have assumed increasing importance.

I have attempted to resolve these internal inconsistencies and theoretical lacunae in a series of three essays (Part I of this volume), each with a different focus. The first deals primarily with the apparent exceptions to the pleasure principle, exceptions that challenge its role as a fundamental principle of psychic behavior. The proposition is offered that *consciousness* provides a principal pathway for psychic discharge. The development of this proposition is complex, since it requires a discussion of some of Freud's early theoretical assumptions in order to demonstrate that they are not consistent with certain clinical observations. The proposed theory of consciousness is a major simplification of metapsychology and provides a good fit with these observations.

The result of this simplification of theory is a general proposition that conceptualizes the essential nature of gratification in the establishment and continued effectiveness of sublimated as well as sexual behavior. A "cycle of satisfaction" describes the nonpathological aspects of psychological functions. This supplements the conflict theory of neurosis and, I believe, broadens the psychoanalytic description of the psychic apparatus.

The second essay introduces Konrad Lorenz's ethological perspective and offers a broader biological base for Freud's theory of instinctual drives. This places aggression on an equal footing with libido in both pathological and nonpathological perspectives. The contributions of the aggressive drive to the normal operations of sublimation and sexual behavior are defined. It is my impression that the delay in the recognition of the importance of aggression during the early history of psychoanalysis is paralleled by the failure of recent theoretical and clinical innovations to acknowledge fully its role in psychopathology.

The third essay integrates these themes with Freud's theory of psychic structure and with the understanding of the affects shame, guilt, and depression. I have made an effort, also, to decrease some of the confusion in psychoanalytic communication occasioned by the frequent redefinition of terms related to "identification."

The functions of gratification and frustration by the analyst of the patient in the therapeutic process have been unclear and at times controversial. This confusion has accompanied the problems of psychoanalytic theory discussed above. In Part II I present three previously published papers that have been edited for inclusion here. In these essays the therapeutic process and psychoanalytic technique are discussed more fully within the framework provided by these theoretical perspectives.

Chapter 7 provides a brief summary of the issues discussed in this work. The reader may wish to read this overview before going on.

Part I

THEORETICAL ASPECTS

1

THE PSYCHOANALYTIC THEORY OF CONSCIOUSNESS

A fundamental technical goal of psychoanalytic treatment is "making the unconscious conscious." Yet Gill and Klein (1967) reported, "Hartmann (personal communication) has said that Freud's inability to solve the problem of quality, that is, the nonquantitative aspects of a structure, was his greatest disappointment, one that made him feel that his theories of consciousness, in their various phases, remained incomplete" (p. 28).

Freud used "consciousness" in three contexts: as the system consciousness of the topographic viewpoint; as a sense organ of the psychic apparatus; and as a quality of a mental operation. My proposal is that psychic discharge is a fundamental requirement for psychic perception and for the function of consciousness as a "sense organ" of the psychic apparatus. "Discharge into consciousness" can be used as a shorthand term for "intrapsychic discharge resulting in a conscious perception," although a neurophysiological construction is not implied. (Nor is it implied that consciousness is the only consequence of psychic discharge.) This reconstruction is more consistent with the development of Freud's theories of psychoanalysis, and with clinical observations, than Freud's early constructions regarding psychic discharge and the economic viewpoint.

The associative process and transference phenomena represent the essential ingredients of psychoanalytic investigation and treatment. These provide the essential observations that are synthesized in the economic viewpoint. Freud described three major exceptions to this viewpoint: sexual excitement, traumatic dreams, and masochism. The challenge to the economic viewpoint provided by these exceptions represents a central issue in clinical psychoanalysis as well as in metapsychology. Two recent panels (Lustman, 1969; Wallerstein, 1977) have revealed a significant trend toward abandonment of the economic viewpoint altogether, and with it, I believe, a cornerstone of psychoanalytic theory and practice. In addition, Gill (1977), who for many years contributed extensively to studies in metapsychology, has recently advocated its abandonment entirely, while Schafer (1976) and Rosenblatt and Thickstun (1977a) have proposed its replacement with entirely different theoretical approaches.

It appears to me that Freud's reconstructions regarding the pleasure principle were hampered by his tendency to intermix clinical observation with metapsychological speculation (see Schur, 1966, for a discussion of this issue). The apparent inconsistencies in the economic viewpoint can be resolved if the two levels of abstraction are not confused. I believe that the solution will provide a more successful integration of clinical observations with theoretical formulations and will help to clarify the roles of gratification and frustration in the psychic economy.

Consciousness

The concept of psychic discharge is closely related to the pleasure principle. The latter expresses an equation between pleasure, or relief of tension, and discharge. Freud (1940) wrote that "the raising of these [instinctual] tensions is in general felt as unpleasure and their lowering as pleasure" (p. 146).

That is, the pleasure principle states that psychic discharge and subjective pleasure, including relief of tension, are parallel phenomena that are dealt with on different levels of abstraction, the metapsychological and the clinical, respectively. In that sense, the subjective experiences of pleasure and unpleasure provide the foundation for understanding the operations of the psychic apparatus.

It appears to me that Freud did not maintain the equation between pleasure and discharge in his constructions regarding psychic discharge. Instead he offered two hypotheses, each of which was based on faulty logic. He originally described the psychic apparatus as an open system with psychic discharge directed to the outside of the psychic apparatus: "Affectivity manifests itself essentially in motor (secretory and vasomotor) discharge resulting in an (internal) alteration of the subject's body without reference to the external world; mobility in actions designed to affect changes in the external world" (Freud, 1915c, p. 179).

An examination of these constructs does not support the thesis that the proposed avenues of discharge are consistently related to pleasure or relief of tension. The description of "secretory and vasomotor" discharge was proposed while Freud was still adhering to his earlier theory of anxiety, which he considered at that time to be the result of a transformation of libido dammed up as a result of repression. The physiological accompaniments of anxiety, including tachycardia and perspiration, were represented as principal avenues of discharge of the repressed libidinal drives.

Anxiety was later redefined as anticipation of the danger of frustration, not as an expression of converted libido (Freud, 1926). Without using the superseded theory of anxiety, we are hard pressed to make the connection between psychic discharge phenomena and the secretory and vasomotor responses which accompany anxiety. In fact, if the physiological accompaniments of anxiety provided avenues of discharge of libido, the affect would provide a homeostatic function, one that would bypass repression and result in relief of tension and conflict. There is no clinical evidence that I know of to support the hypothesis that anxiety or the other tension affects, or even psychosomatic phenomena, provide significant discharge of psychic tension. Only with laughter, crying, and orgasm is there demonstrable evidence of relief of psychic tension consistently accompanying somatic processes. Laughter and crying probably accompany, or "carry," the psychic phenomena into consciousness. It is not clear how the somatic phenomena are related to the psychic, but this does not contradict my thesis. Discharge in sex will be discussed later.

The second concept—discharge by means of action that leads to satisfaction—is logically inconsistent also. For example, if we consider the satisfaction achieved by a child crying for its mother, it is the perception of the mother that produces the lessening of psychic tension. According to Freud, the discharge is defined in terms of the preceding action. It is clear, however, that while action may *lead to* a condition that will provide pleasure, it does not in itself define the condition for pleasure. There may of course be some relief of tension in the act of crying, related to the accompanying conscious fantasy associated with the desired satisfaction, but Freud's construction does not define the intrapsychic situation that would result in such relief. Rather, it expresses the thesis that the condition for discharge and satisfaction is pursued in the external world.

Freud seems to have skirted the idea of discharge into consciousness in the original development of his thesis. In chapter 7 of *The Interpretation of Dreams*, Freud (1900) described the dominant current of the psychic apparatus as directed toward a "perceptual identity"—that is, "a repetition of the perception which was linked with the [earlier] satisfaction of the need" (p. 566). At this point it appears that Freud meant that the dominant trend of the psychic apparatus was the pursuit of a conscious experience, a perception.

Freud then proceeded with the development of a theory of secondary process. He used a construction of "hallucinatory wish-fulfillment"—that might be called a "primitive discharge into consciousness"—as a characteristic of the infantile psychic apparatus. Since this does not achieve the desired satisfaction, he added that

> it is necessary to bring regression to a halt before it becomes complete, so that it does not proceed beyond the mnemic image, and is able to seek out other paths which lead eventually to the desired perceptual identity being established from the direction of the external world. . . . But all the complicated thought-activity which is spun out from the mnemic image to the moment at which the perceptual identity is established by the external world—all this activity of thought merely constitutes a roundabout path to wish-fulfilment which has been made necessary by experience. Thought is after all nothing but a substitute for a hallucinatory wish. . . . [pp. 566–567]

All of this "roundabout" activity directed toward a perceptual identity encompasses the second pathway in Freud's description of the pleasure principle. It is not apparent to me why he abandoned the concept of "perceptual identity" as the condition for satisfaction, with its implication of psychic discharge, in his theory formation. Instead Freud offered an element from the theoretical development of secondary process that described the *pursuit* of satisfaction, rather than the condition for satisfaction and psychic discharge itself.

Later in chapter 7 Freud wrote,

> Dreaming has taken on the task of bringing back under
> control of the preconscious the excitation of the *Ucs.*
> which has been left free; in so doing, it discharges the
> *Ucs.* excitation, serves it as a safety valve and at the same
> time preserves the sleep of the preconscious in return
> for a small expenditure of waking activity. [p. 579]

This description suggests that when the dream "discharges
the *Ucs.* excitation" it utilizes a pathway into consciousness
which is experienced as the manifest dream. This provides
a relief of tension, a decrease in the intensity of the excitation, and permits sleep to continue. The idea of discharge
into consciousness in dreams provides the prototype for
my theory of consciousness.

Certainly, it appears to offer nothing new to suggest
that only those psychological derivatives that have access
to consciousness can provide pleasure or relief of psychic
tension. The major work of psychoanalytic treatment,
making the unconscious conscious, demonstrates that
those instinctual derivatives that do not maintain access to
consciousness are unable to participate freely in pleasure
or relief of tension. It seems to come as a new discovery,
however, to suggest that this ubiquitous psychoanalytic
observation can define the condition for psychic discharge.

Once we acknowledge the logic of the concept of "perceptual identity" as the clinical indicator of psychic discharge, consciousness—rather than affects and action—falls
into place as the expression of discharge. Psychic discharge, then, may be construed as an intrapsychic event.
It can be defined as the alteration of the quantity of energy
of some part of the psychic apparatus from a greater to
a lesser potential, with a resulting effect on the *psychic* environment. This effect commonly involves a conscious perception.

It seems to me that Sandler (1976) may be thinking of something similar when he writes,

> Of particular importance was the view of the role of the dream as a form of surface "expression," a derivative of impulses and wishes moving from the depths to the surface. This view of derivatives of unconscious forces and content can be regarded as a *centrifugal* one, a reflexion of forces moving outwards towards the periphery of the mental apparatus, consistent with the theory of energy "discharge." [p. 37]

It is most important that the technical goal of the therapeutic process, making the unconscious conscious, is consistent with the discharge hypothesis I have proposed. Freud (1915b) held that *"the essence of repression lies simply in turning something away, and keeping it at a distance, from the conscious"* (p. 147). He went on to say, "it is a question of calling a halt when the cathexis of the unconscious reaches a certain intensity—an intensity beyond which the unconscious would break through to satisfaction" (p. 150).

This "breakthrough to satisfaction" is, inevitably, a conscious perception of a fantasy or impulse related to the past. That is, the conscious recollection represents a "perceptual identity" with an earlier wish that is associated with anxiety or guilt. Once repression is overcome and this wish becomes conscious, it may lead to a pleasurable fantasy, like any other "day dream." For example, a patient overcame his conflicts associated with sibling rivalry sufficiently to fantasize consciously that he was the analyst's favorite patient, the only one that "really mattered." The defensive function was clear, not only to avoid anxiety but for relieving tension associated with childhood memories of frustration and loss.

Both day dreams and sleep dreams, therefore, demonstrate phenomena consistent with the hypothesis that fantasies can follow pathways to consciousness that relieve psychic tension. To this must be added that each conscious perception has unconscious connections that are psychodynamically determined. Novey (1958) proposed such an idea when he said that Freud "did not . . . definitely state the theorem that seems most logical: that all sensation, whether from our sense organs or from our inner experience, goes through an unconscious phase before it appears in consciousness and only then do we have the experience of awareness of such sensation" (p. 67).

This psychic process must be identical with the manner in which the dream-work utilizes day residues for discharge of unconscious elements in the manifest dream. Waking external and internal perceptions, therefore, operate in the same manner as the day residues in dreams, providing pathways for discharge of unconscious stimuli on their way to becoming conscious perceptions. In the waking state, this takes place without the abandonment of reality-testing operations, as occurs in dreams.

The concept of the unconscious, in this context, is more comprehensive than that suggested by its relationship to the mechanism of repression. It must include the roots of conflict-free instinctual derivatives just as they are often clearly represented in manifest dreams.

My reconstructions are also consistent with Freud's statement (1923) that "only something that has once been a conscious perception can be conscious again." The inference to be drawn is that the earliest satisfactions of the infant, the direct gratifications of the primitive instinctual needs, establish the primordial pathways to consciousness. That is, when a primary instinctual impulse is satisfied, the resulting memory of satisfaction provides the "content" or "form" to the resulting instinctual "wish." This "wish" represents an essential modification of instinctual drives and establishes a conflict-free point of attachment for later perceptions, unless limited by the development of neurotic conflict.

Both psychic and physical pain can also fit into this psychological scheme. If each perception makes contact with unconscious connections in its path to consciousness, the same could be said about pain. The general statement that this provides a discharge, and therefore relief of tension, presents no problem, since it is such a common observation that human experience is regularly a combination of pleasure and pain in varying proportions. We can still rely on Freud's formulation (1923) that physical pain is dealt with like a psychic tension state, demanding relief in accordance with the pleasure principle.

The concept of "attention" can also be brought into the framework provided by these formulations. Freud (1900) originally included "attention" along with the economic considerations regarding the "system Consciousness." It was inevitable that these constructions would become obsolete when the structural viewpoint essentially replaced the topographic.

Descriptively, "attention" involves the selection of stimuli from the preconscious and from the external world for conscious perception. According to these propositions the selection results in a discharge into consciousness. If we consider the preconscious excitations available for discharge into consciousness, those stimuli in the external world with which they may be associatively connected by prior experience provide important stimuli for this selective process.

Associative connections among preconscious ideas represent preconscious thought. Memories of prior experiences influence both the content of thought as well as the functional integrity of the ego in its pursuit of satisfaction. The ego thus functions as a valve, permitting discharges into consciousness on the basis of the nature and intensity of inner excitations as well as stimuli from the external world. Attention is an expression of the ego's activities involved in providing pathways for psychic discharge.

Conscious thought can then be described as a "mini-discharge," consistent with Freud's designation (1911) of "trial action." It represents a gradient in the psychic apparatus from preconscious to conscious, anticipating greater discharge phenomena. As trial action, conscious thought has the primary function of the pursuit of a "perceptual identity" with an earlier experience of satisfaction. This represents secondary process thought.

The Pleasure Principle

The next task will be to demonstrate that the proposed theory of consciousness does, in fact, resolve the apparent inconsistencies associated with the pleasure principle. Once this is accomplished the economic viewpoint will be established on a more solid footing. According to Freud, the pleasure principle is contradicted by observations of sexual foreplay, masochism, and traumatic neurosis. Clinical observations have clarified a significant part of this problem and will be described briefly before I go on to discuss the role of the theory of consciousness in removing the remaining contradictions.

An expanding literature on the subject of masochism has integrated this clinical phenomenon with other neurotic compromises that are consistent with the pleasure principle (e.g., Berliner, 1958; Socarides, 1958; Spiegel, 1978). Berliner suggested that some of the confusion regarding masochism was associated with Freud's speculations (1924a) regarding the death instinct and his effort to explain the clinical phenomenon of masochism with a biological speculation. Berliner observed clinically that masochism involves a relationship with a sadistic person whose love is needed. Its genesis involves a relationship with a severely depriving or overtly cruel parent. Berliner noted that "the masochistic attitude is the bid for the affection of a hating love object" (p. 41) and that suffering is the price paid for maintaining the attachment. He concluded that "the goal of the masochistic defense . . . is not suffering but the avoidance of suffering" (pp. 44–45).

These observations, along with other formulations of the defensive functions of masochism, are consistent with the pleasure principle.

The clinical literature regarding psychoanalytic observations of traumatic neurosis is less extensive, probably because, in its severe form, it is frequently a manifestation of an ego disorder unsuitable for psychoanalytic investigation. Freud (1919) himself suggested that traumatic neurosis might be classified as an ego disorder, but later (Freud, 1920) discussed the repetitious dreams of traumatic neurosis among his efforts to justify his theory of the death instinct. There, as with the topic of masochism, he ended up with a mixture of clinical observation and metapsychological speculation.

My own observation of patients with traumatic neuroses supports the view that the precipitating trauma rekindled repressed memories of real or fantasied traumatic experiences of childhood. These repressed memories seemed, inevitably, to reflect major frustrations or the fulfillment of forbidden wishes. The traumatic dreams, like other psychological symptoms, appeared to represent repetitious efforts to discharge the tension mobilized by the precipitating event, but could not succeed because of unconscious conflicts.

Although my observations of these patients were not made in formal psychoanalytic treatment, there was, in my opinion, sufficient inferential evidence to support the conclusion that the traumatic events disrupted fragile ego defenses. The traumatic events mobilized infantile conflicts that provided the latent content for the recurrent traumatic dreams. This reconstruction does not require an exception to the pleasure principle.

Freud's speculations concerning traumatic neurosis required the application of the theory of the death instinct, a biological construct, as an explanatory concept for a clinical phenomenon. Thus adequate separation of different hierarchical levels of explanation was not maintained. If there is validity to the concept of a death instinct, its influence should be demonstrable by examination of psychoanalytic data, not by speculations regarding clinical phenomena independent of psychoanalytic observation.

The third and most important challenge to the pleasure principle is the observation that in sexual foreplay the *increase* in sexual tension is experienced as pleasure. The theory of consciousness is indispensable for bringing this observation into the domain of the pleasure principle.

In the sexual sphere, somatic responses are dependent upon psychological stimuli, but these responses—those which participate in the physical excitement—reciprocally intensify the psychological responses. The psychological factors available for this interaction were described by Freud (1905): "Forepleasure is thus the same pleasure that has already been produced, although on a smaller scale, by the infantile sexual instinct" (p. 210).

According to the theory of consciousness, foreplay mobilizes derivatives of the component instinctual drives that Freud referred to, for release into consciousness. This provides pleasure while it triggers the somatic responses which in turn intensify the conscious perceptions and increase the pleasure.

The somatic responses, consequently, provide two psychological contributions to sexual activity. First, they stimulate discharges into consciousness of perceptions from the primary and secondary sex organs as well as from autonomic nervous responses. These accompany and intensify the conscious and unconscious fantasies that have their roots in the early history of the component instincts. Secondly, the somatic tension states are regularly experienced as psychic urges demanding relief, somewhat along the lines of pain reactions.

This aspect of the increase of somatic tension is a crucial issue. Is there sufficient justification for separating two subjective elements in sexual excitement, pleasure and an *accompanying painful* urgency for relief? If we focus on the subjective response to an unwelcome interruption of sexual activity, we are forced to recognize an unpleasurable quality in this urgency for relief. The pleasure responses are no longer stimulated, and the painful urgency stands alone. To the extent that the sexual activity and excitement mobilize pleasurable discharges into consciousness, the experience is predominantly one of pleasure; otherwise, there is uncomfortable tension.

As orgasm is approached during coitus, the somatic responses become more prominent. The physical tension is experienced as a psychological need that is satisfied by physical discharge in the orgasm. The nearer an interruption is to orgasm, the more the tension is experienced as unpleasure.

Furthermore, it is a common observation that high levels of sexual tension are experienced as a kind of discomfort, except during the sexual act. Certainly, our patients often confuse their descriptions of their sexual experiences, but it is not difficult to separate the pleasant anticipation of sexual relief from the sexual tension itself.

It merely suggests the obvious to postulate that there is a specific ego response that permits appropriate stimuli to trigger the somatic sexual responses. Exactly how this is mediated is not clear. The mature ego is able to utilize its capacities for perception, reality testing, and judgment in order to influence release in sexual activity of the instinctual drives.

Gratification and Frustration

The pleasure principle has been justified as a primary quality of the psychic apparatus. Now the essential role of frustration in normal psychological development must be integrated with the theory of the primacy of the pleasure principle. Again, the integration of clinical phenomena with metapsychology must clearly demarcate the clinical and theoretical levels of conceptualization. I will begin with a review of Freud's logic in his effort to integrate the role of frustration with the development of secondary process.

Freud (1900) initially proposed that frustration represents the cardinal experience in the development of secondary process. "The bitter experience of life," he wrote, "must have changed . . . primitive thought-activity into a more expedient secondary one" (p. 566). This conception created a theoretical dilemma: the primary regulatory principle was the pursuit of pleasure or the reduction of unpleasure, but the maturing infant developed the capacity for this pursuit in the real world primarily as a result of frustration of his earliest needs. In view of the importance of gratification to the development of the infant, Freud's reconstruction must be recognized as an assumption that frustration rather than gratification is the essential primary stimulus for the development of what was later called ego development. Parallel with this, Freud observed that frustration was an essential factor in the development of neurosis, an observation that does not fit comfortably alongside his theoretical assumption.

There is another way to reconstruct the roles of gratification and frustration in early development, one that is more consistent with observations. As we have seen, in his speculations regarding the path to the development of secondary process, Freud described an intermediary step of "hallucinatory wish-fulfilment." Freud postulated that the failure to achieve the desired satisfaction by this means—that is, the accompanying frustration—provided the stimulus for the development of secondary process and the pursuit of satisfaction in the external world. It is a simple expedient to alter the focus and recognize that the "hallucination" describes a memory of satisfaction, but unaccompanied by reality testing. Might it not be proper to focus on the memory of prior satisfaction as the stimulus *also* for the thought processes that might lead to relief of tension along a path already traveled? Even if there is an intermediary state of hallucinatory wish-fulfillment, can secondary process along with the capacity for reality testing ever develop without a memory of satisfaction? If not, we are on safe ground if we pursue the question of whether the experiences of satisfaction stimulate the development of the foundations of the ego, a hypothesis that I think is more in keeping with our knowledge of the importance of the gratifying mother in early ego development. The increase of tension that stimulates the hallucinatory experience might then provide the stimulus to utilize the primitive nucleus of the ego, that which is associated with the memory of satisfaction, in the pursuit of relief of tension. That is, the memory of satisfaction provides the kernel of reality testing and tolerance of delay.

We can add to this the knowledge that gratification is essential in order to sustain a functioning, intact ego. In the absence of adequate sources of satisfaction, either because of external deprivation or internal conflict, a sequence of boredom, neurosis, and eventual deterioration of ego functions may occur.

A corollary to the pleasure principle, therefore, sug-

gests itself: The foundations of the ego derive from gratifications of the primordial infantile needs, and the
functional integrity of the ego develops and is sustained
by repeated satisfactions of the psychological derivatives
of those needs. This expresses a restatement of the pleasure principle in terms of structural theory. A shorthand
term for this process is "the cycle of satisfaction."

This brings us up against two crucial observations: it
appears that excessive gratification results in disturbances
in normal childhood development, while moderate frustration provides essential stimuli for emotional growth. I
believe that the "cycle of satisfaction" provides the essential
theoretical concept that brings these observations into harmony with the pleasure principle. During normal ego development the evolving functions of the ego are reinforced
by pleasurable activities involving those functions. The
"good mother" permits and encourages the child to per-
form the activities and establish the controls that are appropriate to its age. The overindulgent mother inhibits
this process and thereby interferes with the growth of age-
appropriate ego functions. She does for the child what the
child should do, and would enjoy doing, for himself, including the mastery of age-appropriate frustration. This
interferes with the satisfactions of instinctual derivatives
that are constantly demanding satisfaction, with the result
that the child's experience is one of relative frustration.
Accordingly, appropriate frustrations actually stimulate
satisfactions—those provided by the cycle of
satisfaction—that are essential for normal development.

A simple example may clarify this issue: A child wants
a cookie before dinner. The mother must either yield or
frustrate the child. It goes without saying that the denial
of the cookie may provide a stimulus for the child's developing capacity to tolerate delay of gratification. The
desire to please the mother, of course, provides the stim-

ulus for the child's *effort* to accept the frustration without excessive anger, as well as to internalize the mother's image into its own developing ego controls. All of this already brings into the scene of frustration the balancing gratifying interaction with the mother. In addition to the desire to please the mother, however, there must be sufficient ego development prior to the incident so that the child is *able to* carry out the desired psychic activity. This involves the prior development of ego capacities that are reinforced by the successful management of the incident. This last item reflects the cycle of satisfaction.

This can be brought into clearer focus by a contrast with the overindulgent mother who believes that her child will benefit from eating large quantities of food. Here the child pleases the mother by eating a proffered cookie. The system of ideals provided by the mother are reinforced by the incident, but there is no reinforcement of the emerging ego functions involved in tolerance of delay and the development of personal autonomy. The cycle of satisfaction is not stimulated, and essential ego functions do not develop from the encounter. The child is infantilized: that is, instinctual derivatives create increasing levels of tension that are dealt with unsuccessfully by overeating.

There is one more issue that falls into place as a result of these considerations regarding the cycle of satisfaction. It is *not* the function of the psychic apparatus to keep the "quantity of excitation" as low as possible, or to keep it constant. The metapsychological formulation that *discharge* of instinctual drive tension is equated with satisfaction implies that it is the discharge phenomenon that is pursued; and this implies the need for challenge and the buildup of psychic tension. Not only in sexual activity, but in theater and music as well as other forms of creative activity, the buildup of tension is an essential ingredient; and if it is interrupted, the affect is unpleasant. Likewise, the "foreplay" in both provides satisfaction associated with "discharges" of accessory impulses that are present and available.

Summary of the Theory of Consciousness

I have addressed the problems of the economic viewpoint that have provoked serious challenges to Freud's metapsychology. These difficulties, I believe, have resulted in large part from a failure to maintain a clear separation of clinical and metapsychological levels of observation and abstraction. The subjective phenomena of pleasure and unpleasure (or pain) provide the clinical bases of observation; while the pleasure principle is a metapsychological concept that derives from, but is not identical with, the clinical phenomena.

A psychodynamic theory of consciousness is proposed that psychic discharge is a fundamental requirement for psychic perception and for the function of consciousness as a "sense organ" of the psychic apparatus. This theory parallels Freud's crucial observations of the wish-fulfilling (discharge) function of the manifest dream and is derived from his theoretical discussion of the dream-work. It solves the economic problem of the pleasure of the increase of sexual tension within the theoretical framework of the pleasure principle. Also, it removes the inconsistencies associated with Freud's theories of psychic discharge that were formulated within the metapsychological framework of the obsolete theories of anxiety and the topographic viewpoint. My theory of consciousness proposes that psychic discharge operates as an intrapsychic phenomenon rather than through vasomotor phenomena and action.

The roles of gratification and frustration in normal childhood development, especially the function of moderate frustration as a stimulus for emotional development, is demonstrated to be consistent with the pleasure principle. A "cycle of satisfaction" summarizes the metapsychological perspective: the foundations of the ego derive from gratifications of the primordial infantile needs, and the functional integrity of the ego develops and is sustained by repeated satisfactions of the psychological derivatives of those needs. Moderate frustration during childhood development is an essential stimulus for the operation of this process. The roles of gratification and frustration as essential components of the therapeutic process in psychoanalysis may also be delineated within this theoretical perspective.

2

Aggression and Sublimation: An Integration of Psychoanalysis and Ethology

The struggle against man's aggressive and destructive tendencies defines not only a major aspect of neurotic disorders but of the history of civilized man as well. Both Konrad Lorenz and Sigmund Freud have given special attention to these issues in their respective fields of study, the former in his formulation of an aggressive instinct in the animal kingdom, the latter in his formulation of an aggressive drive in man. These theoretical perspectives have contributed to the study of how various species, including man, have attempted to contain their potentialities for violence in their relations with other members of their species.

I believe that there is ample justification for introducing an ethological perspective into psychoanalytic discourse regarding the subject of aggression. It is man's aggressive and destructive tendencies that reminds us of our animal status, even while their displacements contribute to the creativity that sets us apart from the remainder of the animal kingdom. Lorenz described the displacement of aggression and its ritualization in the "bond behavior" of a number of species as an important evolutionary adaptation contributing to survival. Freud, by contrast, described aggression as a predominantly destructive force controlled by other psychological forces. Both have been strongly criticized for these theories. Their positive integration, however, may contribute to the validation of both theories and offer an additional biological perspective to traditional Freudian psychoanalysis. A clarification and simplification of both clinical and metapsychological concepts will also emerge from this study.

Darwin has been credited as the originator of ethology, the comparative study of animal behavior, and with providing it an evolutionary impetus (see Lorenz, 1965b). It is interesting to contemporary psychoanalysts to recognize the prophetic quality of Darwin's theorizing about man, especially the similarity of some of his ideas to Freud's theory of psychic energy. Darwin (1872) wrote that

> experience shows that nerve-force is generated and set free whenever the cerebro-spinal system is excited. The direction which this nerve-force follows is necessarily determined by the lines of connection between the nerve-cells, with each other and with various parts of the body. But the direction is likewise much influenced by habit [experience]; inasmuch as nerve-force passes readily along accustomed channels. [p. 348]

According to Kramer (1977), another ethologist, neurophysiology has failed to provide a biological foundation for psychiatry, specifically because of

> the failure of this discipline to recognize the biological fact that animals are unable to move individual muscles, let alone a motor unit (a single nerve fiber and the muscle fibers it serves). Nervous systems only can initiate patterns of movement. Ethologists have termed these units of behavior *fixed motor patterns* in recognition of the fact they represent inherited, not learned, units of behavior, which are structured in the neuromuscular system of animals and are subject to evolution. [p. 78]

Environmental stimuli are necessary to release these fixed motor patterns. The releasing stimuli as well as the fixed motor patterns are species specific.

In a statement that appears to update Darwin's ideas, Kramer added,

> If we translate our ethological concepts into psychoanalytic terminology, the infant's id functions (all that is instinctive) can only be carried out by means of its fixed motor patterns, while the fate, or experience, of those motor patterns in the outside world (the individual way in which they are combined, integrated, or inhibited), makes up its ego structure (all that is experiential). [p. 102]

Freud's attempt to pursue a biological orientation was bound to fail as long as he depended on an inadequate neurophysiological model, as he did in the seventh chapter of *Interpretation of Dreams* (Freud, 1900). The development of his structural theory, however, provided the theoretical perspective that could be integrated with ethological studies. It was not mere coincidence, I think, that this theoretical development occurred once Freud's attention became increasingly focused on problems of aggression.

Freud's personal history led him to focus on conflicts associated with sexuality for many years before he accorded to problems of aggression the attention they deserved. Only later, evidently stimulated by the horrors of World War I, did his clinical studies and theoretical speculations lead him to acknowledge the major role played by aggression in man's psychic economy, a task he was able to accomplish only with great difficulty (Schur, 1972). It was also about this time that Freud recognized the significance of unconscious resistances, with the result that exclusive reliance on the topographical theory became obsolete. These two developments provided the basis, not only for further clinical investigation, but for a biological integration that was less inhibited by Freud's neurophysiological bias.

Freud's initial approach to the problem of an aggressive drive—*Beyond the Pleasure Principle* (1920)—was intermingled with philosophical speculation and undefined metapsychological constructions. In particular, Freud sidestepped his clinical observations regarding the role of neurotic conflict in the repetitious expression of infantile needs and fantasies in the transference. Instead, in one of his most speculative papers, he described the "repetition compulsion" as an expression of, and a justification for, his formulation of a "death instinct." Freud was aware of these difficulties, however, and he added,

> in any case it is impossible to pursue an idea of this kind except by repeatedly combining factual material with what is purely speculative and thus diverging widely from empirical observation. The more frequently this is done in the course of constructing a theory, the more untrustworthy, as we know, must be the final result. [1920, p. 59]

I think that most Freudian analysts now understand the persistence of infantile fantasies and their repetition in the transference to be the result of neurotic defenses that sustain the conflict. That is, unconscious sources of anxiety provide the stimuli for the maintenance of ego defenses and prevent the resolution of conflict on a contemporary level (Freud, 1926). The greater awareness of problems of aggression and their role in neurosis does not require the assumption of a death instinct. The systematic clinical focus on the ego's defensive operations during psychoanalytic treatment (e.g., as discussed by Glover, 1955), regularly mobilizes conflicts surrounding aggressive impulses and permits their analysis. Successful psychoanalysis leads to amelioration of the neurotic compulsion to repeat the past with its accompanying frustrations.

I believe that the topic of sublimation provides an essential focus for a more thorough psychoanalytic study of aggression and for its integration with ethological theory. Though Lorenz (1963) anticipated that the psychoanalytic study of sublimation would contribute to solving the dilemma of unbridled aggression in man, his own attempt foundered on his inability to differentiate the homeostatic roles of neurosis and sublimation. This no doubt reflected similar difficulties that Freud himself displayed in dealing with this issue.

Clinical Disparities

It would be most desirable if contemporary psychoanalysts did not have to repeat Freud's trials and errors but could instead mature in their scientific development on the foundations he provided. Segments of the psychoanalytic community, however, regress periodically as new theories are proposed that obscure the clinical significance of problems of aggression. Lewy (1941) has described the tendency of some members of the analytic community to abandon the hard-won gains of psychoanalytic observations and to rationalize these regressions with new theoretical and technical formulations. At the time he wrote it was the libido theory and the clinical significance of sexuality that was under attack. He commented, "We believe this kind of theory revision can properly be called 'acting out' in the same sense as we see it in our analytic patients" (p. 48).

It is beyond the scope of the present work to criticize in depth the various schools of thought that have arisen during the past forty years, but I wish to describe how some of the reconstructions designed to reinterpret or replace Freudian metapsychology have tended to obscure

clinical problems related to aggression (for further discussion of this point, see chapter 6).

Lipton (1977) has described distortions of Freud's technique by certain authors who asserted a "classical" Freudian technique. A misunderstanding of the "rule of
abstinence" evidently provided the impetus for the abandonment of the primary focus on interpretation of de-
fense/resistance. Instead, the analyst's silence was
conceptualized as a primary instrument for mobilizing a
regressed transference neurosis. As a result, resistances
against primitive aggression were not adequately confronted and the resulting idealized transference phenomena defended against the analysis of major areas of
neurotic conflict, especially those potentially expressed by
hostile transference fantasies.

Rothstein (1980) has observed that Goldberg's reports
(1978) of patients treated in accordance with Kohut's theories revealed, among other deficiencies, unresolved problems related to sadomasochistic fantasies. The systematic
interpretation of narcissistic defenses ordinarily mobilizes
conflicts associated with primitive aggression. Kohut's in-
sistence that narcissistic phenomena observed in the transference be treated as residual deficiency states from
infantile development, rather than as neurotic defenses,
prevents the investigation of repressed impulses and fantasies.

Kohut's recommended technique places exaggerated
emphasis on "empathy" as a therapeutic modality. He
minimizes the importance of resistance interpretation, with
the result that his technique provides a counterresistance
against mobilizing primitive hostility.

Kleinian theory bypasses the issue of interpretation of
defense/resistance in a direct manner with the admonition
that the *deepest* levels of infantile fantasies must be interpreted first. The result is that the ego defenses manifested

in the patient's resistances are ignored. This is a paradoxical situation, since Kleinian theory places so much emphasis on primitive destructive fantasies, especially in the theoretical constructions of the schizoid position. Furthermore, in the hands of skillful therapists clinically significant aggressive and destructive fantasies are mobilized. However, the full impact of the aggressive affect is avoided. This weakness is rationalized by a fundamental assumption, one that denies the significance of the tension state associated with the hostile affects. Segal (1964), a dedicated follower of Klein, wrote, "In Melanie Klein's view, unconscious phantasy is the mental expression of instincts, and therefore, like these, exists from the beginning of life" (p. 2).

Fairbairn's theory, like Klein's, is based on the assumption that affects are manifested by the accompanying fantasy, and again provides an effective basis for the analyst's counterresistances against the analysis of primitive expressions of hostile aggression. This problem exists even though Fairbairn's theory, like Klein's, describes major problems related to aggression. Guntrip (1961), Fairbairn's advocate and interpreter, wrote, "When analysis has the chance to go deep enough it is truly astonishing how powerful and frightening to·the patient is the degree of primitive infantile rage, unsatisfied need and intense fear-ridden dependent longing that is revealed" (p. 390).

I have observed in clinical conferences presenting Fairbairn's approach, including some conducted by Guntrip, that specific but theoretically determined destructive fantasies were regularly interpreted. The affects—the hostility and the associated anxiety—were not confronted. This regularly reinforced the intellectual defenses, relieved the patient's anxiety temporarily, and removed the hostile impulses from the arena of the transference.

Rosenblatt and Thickstun (1977b) have asserted that

Freud's metapsychology is obsolete and have suggested its replacement with a cognitive-motivational model of the psychic apparatus. They rationalize abandonment of the dynamic and economic viewpoints on the basis of their flagrant abuse, an argument that could justify the abandonment of psychoanalysis altogether.

Freud's metapsychology is based on the essential data derived from the psychoanalytic system of observation. In their criticism of metapsychology, Rosenblatt and Thickstun fail to take into account the essential links between metapsychology and clinical psychoanalysis. They have apparently confused the fundamental analogies of metapsychology with Freud's more speculative and metaphorical discussions regarding their theoretical significance.

In an earlier paper, Rosenblatt and Thickstun (1970) wrote that "the elements for substitute paradigms are now available. The resultant theoretical changes could be incorporated in the body of analytic theory without sacrifice of the fundamental concepts most closely related to clinical observation" (p. 272). In a later paper, however, they recommended the replacement of the dynamic-economic viewpoints with a theory of "motivational systems" about which they acknowledged, "We recognize not only the imprecision of such a definition, but also the difficulty in selecting appropriate terms for a concept whose limits and applications are yet to be thoroughly explored" (1977b, p. 109).

Rosenblatt and Thickstun attempted to rationalize their effort to relegate affects to a secondary role by means of a computer model. Although they stated, "It must here be emphasized that, in discarding the dynamic point of view, we are not in any way ignoring or minimizing the role of affect," they added, "Affect is conceptualized as a phase of a vital appraisal process, operating as a feedback loop in all but the simplest behavioral systems" (p. 109).

Affects are the essential guidelines that validate the investigation of unconscious processes. They represent the conscious manifestations of the "power" or "force" that Rosenblatt and Thickstun would replace with a concept of "metabolic energy." This is a clinical issue, not a theoretical one.

All of these theoretical revisions that diminish the role of aggressive affects relate to one essential clinical phenomenon: the experience of a specific subjective tension that is recognized as a manifestation of a hostile aggressive affect such as anger or rage. Only when this is experienced by the patient can there be any sense of conviction—by patient or analyst—of the validity of the phenomenon. The fact that the patient may join the analyst in recognizing convincing *evidence* of the affect or its associated fantasies should not be confused with the actual emergence of the affect into consciousness. Hostile aggressive tension states are primarily defended against, since they are most intimately associated with an urge for action with its accompanying fear of consequences, and they carry the most significant memories of infantile frustration. The verbal expression of the accompanying thought or fantasy has an intrusive or explosive quality unless inhibited by anxiety, guilt, or shame. The emergence of the tension often carries the associated fantasies or ideas into consciousness from their preconscious or unconscious roots. The process of working through requires repeated confrontations of conflicts associated with these affects.

Let me give a clinical example. A forty-year-old depressed woman, in psychoanalysis for slightly over a year, had developed a strong attachment to me. This had stimulated her to reexamine her relationship with her husband. Her projections of hostility and contempt were repeatedly recognized and interpreted as manifestations of splitting. That is, she defended against the ambivalence in the transference by splitting off the hostility to her husband and rationalized it by projecting it onto him. She repeatedly asserted, without apparent justification, that he felt a great deal of hostility toward her. This early investigation resulted in a marked improvement in her relationship with her husband. Her sexual responses intensified, and her husband responded in kind. At the same time, her "oral" cravings increased and became an obsession. This could be relieved only for a short time by fellatio.

The patient became aware of fears of being abandoned by both her husband and me, and this was increasingly associated with her father's emotional detachment and rejecting behavior toward her. She recalled vague feelings of guilt, at first experienced as guilt over "wanting too much."

Near the beginning of the second year of analysis the patient reported a "frightening" incident with her husband. The bedroom was cold, she said, and she had invited him to indulge in some playful "roughhousing" in order to "warm up." As they were enjoying this, something "came over" her, she let out an angry yell and became extremely frightened. She said that she "put the controls back" instantly, and she reassured her husband that he had not made her angry.

As she focused on the incident, she recognized that she had "lost control" over "vicious" feelings that she had not previously experienced. Now she began to work through the affective aspects of the hostile fantasies that had been an important focus of the analysis until then. Her "oral" obsession became less intense, and the patient's collaboration in the analysis took on a new meaning. She began to experience, for the first time, her intensely ambivalent feelings toward me. For example, she began a subsequent session very emotionally, with assertions of hating me, complaints about my fee, and allegations that I was indifferent to her feelings. Near the end of the hour she burst into tears and said that she loved me very much.

Such clinical phenomena correlate with Freud's definition: "quota of affect . . . corresponds to the instinct insofar as the latter has become detached from the idea and finds expression, proportionate to its quantity, in processes which are sensed as affects" (1915b, p. 152).

The various manifestations of hostility represent tension affects in contradistinction to pleasure affects. Any approach that denies such tension phenomena as fundamental observations has an entirely inadequate clinical basis and can only lead to unsatisfactory results.

It is my suggestion that sublimations incorporate a species-specific biological discharge of aggression that was developed in the course of human evolution, and that other manifestations of displacement of aggression, those similar to what we observe in other species, do not have the same homeostatic effect in man. The issue has been clouded by the fact that the prolonged childhood development of sublimations frequently results in disturbances in their functions and in their becoming the tools of destructiveness. If we examine clinically the normal operation of sublimations in man, however, and compare them with the species-specific safeguards Lorenz has described in animals, I think that their common functions will be recognized.

Lorenz's Observations on Aggression

Lorenz designated aggressive behavior by an individual toward other members of its own species as "intraspecific aggression." He described two aspects of this phenomenon: first, its role in preserving the species; and, second, its status as a danger to the species that must be protected against. As a positive force it contributes to a balanced

distribution of animals of the same species over the available environment; it leads to selection of the strongest; and
it is essential in the defense of the young.

On the other hand, this force must be restricted if the
species is to survive. At the very least, intraspecific mechanisms must be established to permit sexual union. Some
species demonstrate additional benefits from this restriction by banding together for protection and for collective
efforts to secure food.

Lorenz addressed the question of the manner in which
the destructive capacities of an aggressive species are controlled in order to prevent its members from destroying
themselves. He described how each species that has evolved
aggressive capabilities in its struggle for survival has also
developed instinctual restraints against aggression directed
toward its own members. These restraints became incorporated into various kinds of social organizations. One
such form of social organization was achieved in the course
of evolution by two developments: the redirection of
aggression and the establishment of "bonds" between individual members of the species. Human society provides
an example of such an organization.

Lorenz (1963) observed that functions associated with
aggression that originally evolved out of the necessity of
coping with the environment later became ritualized as a
means of communication within the species:

> a behavior pattern by means of which a species . . . deals
> with certain environmental conditions, acquires an en-
> tirely new function, that of communication. The primary
> function may still be performed, but it often recedes
> more and more into the background and may disappear
> completely so that a typical change of function is achieved.
> Out of communication two new equally important func-
> tions may arise, both of which still contain some measure
> of communicative effects. The first of these is the chan-

neling of aggression into innocuous outlets, the second
is the formation of a bond between two or more individuals. [p. 72]

Lorenz added, "We know that, in the evolution of verte-
brates, the bond of personal love and friendship was the
epoch-making invention . . . when it became necessary for
two or more individuals of an aggressive species to live
together and to work for a common end" (p. 289). Lorenz
concluded that all "bond behavior" has evolved, by way of
ritualization, on the basis of intraspecific aggression. One
of his most interesting arguments is the observation that
bond behavior exists only in those species that have a high
degree of aggression. Even in those species where seasonal
changes take place with regard to aggressiveness and
schooling or flocking, all individual ties are dissolved when
the organism changes from its aggressive to its nonag-
gressive state.

As an example of bond behavior in a lower species,
Lorenz (1963) described a genus of fish, the Cichlids.

> Pair formation takes place in the following way: on reach-
> ing sexual maturity, a certain fish, usually a male, takes
> possession of a territory and drives out all the others.
> Later, when a female is willing to pair, she approaches
> the territory owner cautiously and, if she acknowledges
> the superior rank of the male, responds to his attacks
> which, at first, are quite seriously meant, . . . with the so-
> called "coyness behavior," consisting . . . of behavior ele-
> ments arising partly from mating and from escape drives.
> If, despite the clearly aggression-inhibiting intention of
> these gestures, the male attacks, the female may leave his
> territory for a short time, but sooner or later she returns.
> This is repeated over a varying period until each of the
> two animals is so accustomed to the presence of the other
> that the aggression-eliciting stimuli inevitably proceeding
> from the female lose their effect. [pp. 161–162]

Lorenz (1964) described how the attachment that develops continues to depend on ritualized aggressive behavior between the animals. This consists in the male repeatedly performing a specific ritual in the presence of its mate.

> The motor elements involved retain the patterns of threat behavior . . . except that they are welded into a fixed sequence and invariably directed, as a final goal, against an object other than the mate. . . . The reliability of the mechanisms deflecting aggression from the mate still hinges in most of the Cichlid species on the possibility of discharging an attack against a hostile neighbor [although generally not to a mortal outcome]. [p. 46]

In the absence of such a neighbor, the mate is in danger of attack.

Lorenz's critics have evidently confused his premise, equating his thesis that "aggression is natural" with "aggression is good." Lorenz's descriptions, however, demonstrate that the aggressive behavior in nonhuman species is adaptive and contributes to survival. He has recently reasserted his view that "aggression—aggressivity—follows all the rules of threshold lowering and appetitive behavior. You can see an animal looking for trouble" (Evans, 1975, p. 38).

Lorenz has also been criticized for his application of the concept of "innate" behavioral responses, based on the alleged difficulty in differentiating such behavior from "learned" behavior. The assumption of such "innate" responses to specific stimuli appears to be essential to the concept of the instinctual roots of aggression. Lorenz has responded to these criticisms in great detail, especially in his monograph, *Evolution and Modification of Behavior* (1965a). A more recent and more summary defense of his view appears in Evans (1975): "if learning improves survival value, the learning apparatus must contain information about what ought to be learned and what ought not to be learned" (p. 81).

The phenomena of ritualized displacement of aggression and accompanying "bonding" occur throughout the animal kingdom, including some higher vertebrate species. Lorenz (1963) observed, however, that the efficient and large-scale destructive capacities developed by man's higher intelligence has jeopardized the rather precarious balance available to him in nature. He went on to speculate that

> all his trouble arises from his being a basically harmless, omnivorous creature, lacking in natural weapons with which to kill his prey, and, therefore, also devoid of the built-in safety devices which prevent "professional" carnivores from abusing their killing power to destroy fellow members of their own species. . . .
>
> In human evolution, no inhibitory mechanisms preventing sudden manslaughter were necessary, because quick killing was impossible anyhow. . . . all of a sudden, the invention of artificial weapons upset the equilibrium of killing potential and social inhibitions. [p. 233]

Lorenz (1964) concluded that

> there cannot be any doubt, in the opinion of any biologically-minded scientist that intraspecific aggression is, in Man, just as much a spontaneous instinctive drive as in most other higher vertebrates. The beginning synthesis between the findings of Ethology and Psychoanalysis does not leave any doubt, either, that what Sigmund Freud has called the death drive is nothing else but the miscarrying of this instinct which, in itself, is as indispensable to survival as any other. [p. 49]

Earlier, Lorenz (1955) had written, "I believe—and

human psychologists, particularly psychoanalysts, should test this—that present-day civilized man suffers from insufficient discharge of his aggressive drive" (p. 235), with the consequence that it is diverted into violence and war.

Aggression and Neurosis

If we were to follow Lorenz's observations to one possible conclusion, it would appear at first as if violence and war are specific safeguards that are necessary to preserve bonds of love and friendship in man, just as the hostile territorial neighbor functions in the bond behavior of the Cichlid. In fact, Lorenz (1963, p. 242) noted that there were certain primitive tribes in Central New Guinea where such a situation still existed. The peaceful coexistence of members within each tribe appeared to be associated with a perennial state of limited warfare with surrounding tribes. Lorenz speculated that civilized man suffers from inadequate means of discharge of aggression that may have been provided by such circumstances.

Can small-scale warfare be the means provided by evolution for the displacement of aggression that is essential for preserving human "bonds," the safety valve that was thrown out of balance by the development of the capacity for mass warfare? This would carry the implication that the displacement of aggression provides an essential and effective means of discharge that is necessary to preserve psychic homeostasis.

This argument might be carried a step further through the consideration that ambivalence is observed to be a major issue in every neurotic symptom, as well as in every personal relationship. Displacements of aggression, both in symptoms and in behavior, would represent a means of coping with ambivalence in such a manner that object relationships are preserved.

Furthermore, all neurotic symptoms and behavior paradoxically manifest a ritualized quality comparable to the ritualized bond behavior of other species. This has been called the "compulsion to repeat." According to Freud, this repetitious quality demonstrates the influence of unneutralized aggression, an inference that led him to his far-reaching speculations regarding the biological nature of aggression in man (Freud, 1937, pp. 242–243). All this supports the argument that *neurosis*—especially as it represents the displacement of aggression—constitutes the ritualized bond behavior of our species, the group of psychological mechanisms that have evolved to preserve the human species against its self-destruction.

This line of reasoning would imply that the therapeutic goals of analysis require the preservation of effective means of discharge of aggression onto scapegoats, limited only by the requirements of reality testing and self-preservation. This is a decisive issue, I believe. The release of aggressive impulses from their involvements in neurotic symptoms would free them for destructive pursuits, and personal relationships would be preserved to the extent that scapegoats were available. It would mean that we need enemies in order to survive and to maintain our health.

On the contrary, displacements of aggression without neutralization of its destructive quality are expressions of pathological manifestations with limiting effects on interpersonal relationships, the "bond behavior" of man. This is true whether the aggression is "deflected" into neurotic symptoms or into behavior. Neurotic symptoms, like aggressive behavior, contribute to precarious psychic homeostasis, while major areas of psychological functions are withdrawn from close personal relationships. When such behavioral displacements are examined in the analytic setting they inevitably represent defensive processes associated with unresolved conflict. Pathological phenomena of this kind, with their *limiting* effects on human bond behavior, are unlikely candidates to be the prototype of biologically determined safeguards against intraspecific aggression.

A clinical example of this issue is demonstrated by an obsessive-compulsive patient, Mr. A. His neurosis was characterized by an ongoing pursuit of organization, orderliness, and logic. The failure of these defenses was manifested by chronic depressive symptoms as well as coprophilic obsessions—fantasies of eating the remains of dead animals.

His initial psychiatric consultation, however, was stimulated by the desire for counseling for his failing marriage. He felt that he was unreasonably demanding, angry, and provocative to his wife, and that he shared "equally" in responsibility for their marital problems. Because of a prior experience with psychotherapy he was responsive to the recommendation for psychoanalysis.

The patient's obsessive character traits were supported by idealization of his intellect. Although he began with self-deprecating associations related to his obsessions, his idealization of his intellectual powers soon emerged and was manifested by expressions that he was unique in his knowledge of the way things should be. This was the message to the analyst in his repeated assertions of his own failures.

Interpretations of the defensive nature of his grandiosity led to increasing anger, and after some months of analysis his fear of "losing control" of his destructive impulses became an important issue. Earlier in his marriage, in fact, he had become so enraged with his wife during an argument that he had attempted to strangle her. He had regained his self-control only after he became frightened that he might kill her.

Mr. A claimed that he was appropriately afraid of his rage and fully justified in pursuing his rigid controls. Further investigation revealed the projection of his violent fantasies, their relation to underlying phobias, and a childhood history of fear of his father.

All of this defensive armor failed to help sustain any emotional attachments, and his personal relationships were unsatisfying. During the "courtship" with his future wife he had had sexual relations with many other women in addition to his wife, evidently with her knowledge. He felt emotionally detached at the time of the wedding, and this had persisted to the present. As the analysis progressed and he became able to see his wife more clearly, he recognized for the first time that she hated him as much as he hated her.

The neurotic defenses had failed to prevent the destructive impulses from intruding seriously on his "bond behavior" with his wife. Although scapegoats were available in his work as well as in his personal prejudices, the struggle against his destructive impulses had dominated his existence to such an extent that he was unable to develop or sustain a satisfying personal relationship.

Such clinical observations demonstrate that man's propensity to persecute scapegoats does not need to be elevated to the level of a biological homeostatic mechanism. This report also provides a demonstration of the fact that the superego fails to provide for the effective redirection of aggression. Superego controls represent an "internal" psychic displacement of aggression similar to symptoms, and, like the latter, fail to contribute effectively to man's bond behavior. Mr. A was restrained from acknowledging his hatred of his wife by the punitive aspects of his superego, and it helped prevent him from murdering her. However, it reinforced the obsessive mechanisms which substituted for personal relationships and contributed to their failure.

Those relationships which are motivated by submission

to superego demands lack the quality of affection and empathy that are essential for satisfaction and success. The accusations from the superego that accompany the demands for submission are, inevitably, reflections of the persistent demands of unacceptable or destructive impulses and fantasies. The latter represent a constant threat to personal relationships, and the role of the superego is often limited to punishment after the expression of unacceptable behavior.

In addition, the frequency with which morality and guilt provide the impetus for unrestrained aggression, even for massive warfare, is well known. Lorenz (1963) recognized this limitation in a manner consistent with psychoanalytic understanding when he wrote,

> We have better chances of supporting moral responsibility in its ever-increasing task if we humbly realize and acknowledge that it is "only" a compensating mechanism of very limited strength and that . . . it derives what power it has from the same kind of motivational sources as those which it has been created to control. [p. 246]

Sublimation

Freud arrived at a definition of sublimation before he had modified his theoretical formulations to include the aggressive drive. In his early paper on narcissism Freud (1914b) defined sublimation in the manner that currently is most widely accepted. "Sublimation," he wrote, "is a process that concerns object-libido and consists in the instinct's directing itself towards an aim other than, and remote from, that of sexual satisfaction; in this process, the accent falls upon deflection from sexuality" (p. 94).

After redefining instinctual drive theory to include the aggressive drive, Freud (1923) attempted to describe the vicissitudes of the two drives in the development of the ego and superego. He postulated that sublimation occurred parallel with ego and superego identifications, and that this was accompanied by a defusion of libidinal and aggressive instincts.

> When it happens that a person has to give up a sexual object, there quite often ensues an alteration of his ego which can only be described as a setting up of the object inside the ego. . . . It may be that this identification is the sole condition under which the id can give up its objects. . . .
>
> The transformation of object-libido into narcissistic libido which thus takes place obviously implies an abandonment of sexual aims, a desexualization—a kind of sublimation, therefore. Indeed the question arises, and deserves careful consideration, whether this is not the universal road to sublimation. . . . [pp. 29–30]

To this Freud added, "After sublimation the erotic component no longer has the power to bind the whole of the destructiveness that was combined with it, and this is released in the form of an inclination to aggression and destructiveness" (p. 54). In this description of the development of the superego, Freud hypothesized that sublimations develop by means of identifications as a result of the resolution of the Oedipus complex. By means of his hypothesis that the development of sublimations inevitably releases aggression, Freud could explain the harshness and cruelty of the superego.

Freud (1924b), however, soon added a different perspective regarding the development of the superego:

> But the process we have described is more than a repression. It is equivalent, if it is ideally carried out, to a destruction and an abolition of the complex. We may

> plausibly assume that we have come upon the border-
> line—never a very sharply drawn one—between the nor-
> mal and the pathological. If the ego has in fact not
> achieved much more than a repression of the complex,
> the latter persists in an unconscious state in the id and
> will later manifest its pathogenic effect. [p. 177]

Freud's description of the "borderline" between the normal and the pathological suggests a different reconstruction for the development of sublimations than the one he
suggested in 1923. The "destruction and . . . abolition of
the [Oedipus] complex" does not result in the elimination
of sublimations, but it does remove the "pathogenic" qualities of the harsh superego. There is more likely to be a
negative correlation between the harsh superego and effective sublimations than a positive one. The harsh superego, in fact, intrudes on the effective operations of
sublimated behavior. It is the intensity of the ambivalence
to the father which determines whether effective sublimations will develop or, alternatively, a harsh superego.
Sublimations and the harsh superego therefore represent
identifications with the father which are, respectively, relatively conflict-free or ambivalent. It is necessary to conclude that the harshness and rigidity of the superego, with
all its danger of being redirected outward, reflects the unresolved hatred of the oedipal father which is incorporated
into the superego and turned against the self (or ego),
while sublimations represent the derivatives of the desex-
ualized attachment to the father to the extent that the
Oedipus complex is resolved.

Viewed from the perspective that the development of
sublimations does not release aggression, the role of earlier, preoedipal impulses fits more comfortably into our
theory. Sublimations manifest the derivatives of such early
stages and undoubtedly have their roots in them. These

are modified and reinforced by the identifications associated with the Oedipus complex.

Clinical observations demand this reconstruction. The very extreme qualities of the superego describe a common clinical situation which psychoanalysis attempts to modify, often with substantial success. The result is that the sublimations that derive from early identifications are stabilized. That is, as conflict over ambivalence is diminished, sublimations are reinforced and the superego becomes less harsh and punitive. This is accompanied by the achievement of an increased capacity for object constancy, the conflict-free expression of bond behavior in man. The sublimations become enhanced by an increasing capacity for empathy, while the danger of violence diminishes.

Let me give a brief example of a therapeutic change that illustrates some of these issues. This is such a common result of successful psychoanalytic treatment that a more detailed report seems unnecessary: A young man, Mr. B, presented himself for treatment because of ejaculatio praecox. Information obtained during the course of treatment revealed that he was inhibited from looking at his wife when she was naked, with the result that his voyeuristic impulses were unavailable for sexual foreplay. Secondarily, he described his construction business as one in which he had to cheat in order to meet the competition and make a living, and he wanted the treatment to free him from his guilty conscience.

In the therapeutic setting the patient was unable to look directly at me, and he could glance at me only out of the corners of his eyes when the opportunity was available. During the treatment the patient discovered that looking represented a sadistic attack—"looking with daggers." As he worked through the conflicts associated with his aggressive fantasies, he became capable of enjoying sexual foreplay, his premature ejaculation improved, and his per-

sonal relationships, especially his marriage, were enhanced. Also, the patient developed pride in the more
artistic and creative aspects of his work; and he found that
he was making more money as a result of the improvement
in his work than he had by cheating. The resolution of his
neurosis led to relatively conflict-free sublimations as his
"bond behavior" improved.

The resolution of such conflict can be defined in one
of two ways: either the psychological roots of the sadistic
fantasies no longer exist; or they are diverted from the
neurotic conflict and expressed in other forms of behavior.
The former would imply that anger and sadism, the hostile
manifestations of aggression, are responses to libidinal
frustration exclusively, and that they do not exist in the
absence of such frustration. In that case, its homeostatic
function in the psychic apparatus as well as its adaptive
value would be obscure, since it would be directed primarily toward the elimination of the provider of libidinal
satisfactions.

As we have seen, Mr. B developed new interests in the
artistic and creative aspects of his work, as well as in sexual
foreplay. That is, Freud's therapeutic goal was achieved:
Where id was, there ego shall be. Both spheres, of work
and sexuality, are known to contain roots of nondestructive
aggressive impulses that are subordinated to creative or
productive goals. It is more reasonable to conclude that
the aggressive drive that had participated in the neurotic
conflict was now subordinated to his libidinal needs both
in sexuality and in sublimated behavior. This was accompanied by stabilization of his marriage.

The punitive aspects of Mr. B's superego were also
silenced. "Cheating" had expressed displacements of his
sadistic goals, and these had been redirected at himself by
means of his conscience. This aspect of his punitive conscience was replaced by reasonable ideals that provided

"ego satisfactions." The unconscious image of the punitive, loved-hated father had been replaced by relatively conflict-free identifications.

Sublimation and Defense

Clinical observations offer many examples of the integration of libidinal and aggressive drive derivatives. The mature ego is able to control the conditions which mobilize the somatic sexual responses as well as to divert its goals toward sublimated satisfactions. In the latter case sexual interests are not ordinarily diminished, unless there is an accompanying neurosis. Despite the fact that we have no understanding, at this time, of how this is achieved within the central nervous system, the clinical information must be reflected in our theories. A careful examination of Freud's approach to the theory of sublimation reveals serious confusion with regard to this issue.

When Freud (1905) introduced "sublimation" into psychoanalytic theory, he asked, "What is it that goes to the making of these constructions which are so important to the growth of a civilized and normal individual? They probably emerge *at the cost of* the infantile sexual impulses themselves" (p. 178; italics mine). As Freud clarified the role of sublimation as an alternative to defense, he did not abandon his belief that the sublimated functions were diverted from sexuality. In "An Outline of Psycho-Analysis" (1940) he continued to describe sublimated functions as "excluded from the [genital sexual] organization" (p. 155).

This fallacy also intruded into efforts by later authors to conceptualize the psychology of sublimation. Hartmann (1955) continued Freud's thesis that sublimation "refers to a psychological process, this process being a change in the mode of energy, away from an instinctual and toward a noninstinctual mode" (p. 223).

It is a conceptual fallacy that adult manifestations of sexuality are instinctual while sublimations are not. The infant can neither sublimate nor copulate. Both potentialities develop out of psychological inborn predispositions.

Freud carried this confusion over into his discussion of "binding." This is a process usually described as an inhibitory influence exerted upon the primary process; it is characteristic of the secondary process and the reality principle (Freud, 1900, pp. 599–601). That is, it reflects the clinical observation of the development of tolerance for delayed gratification. In *Beyond the Pleasure Principle* (1920) Freud remarked that "there seems to be no doubt whatever that the unbound or primary processes give rise to more intense feelings in both directions than the bound or secondary ones" (p. 63). In the same work, however, only one page earlier, he had written, "The binding of an instinctual impulse would be a preliminary function designed to prepare the excitation for its final elimination in the pleasure of discharge" (p. 62).

If "binding" prepares an impulse for discharge, it would appear that in its "unbound" (primary process) state it would be *less* likely to achieve discharge and acquire intense feelings. Only those childhood needs that are inhibited by neurotic defenses ordinarily retain their "primary process" qualities; and it is precisely those needs that cannot be satisfied. It has become axiomatic that the inability to tolerate delay (represented metapsychologically as the expression of primary process) interferes seriously with a buildup of tension sufficient to provide full satisfaction. The accompanying tension may be prominent, but the pleasurable affects associated with discharge are relatively lacking.

For example, the "oral craving" of an hysterical patient, while allowing some degree of pleasure, cannot lead to satisfaction. Infantile manifestations of instinctual drives that are observed in neurotic conflict are neither more nor less "instinctual" than their derivatives, but they are certainly less available for satisfying discharge in either direction. There is a basic fallacy in the idea that the residues of infantile needs that are observed clinically, and which manifest primary process qualities, are their undistorted instinctual representations; rather, their qualities are in fact determined by their association with memories of childhood frustration.

Freud's alternative hypothesis, that binding prepares for discharge, serves us better. When infantile needs are replaced by mature interests as a result of psychoanalysis, satisfaction becomes available by means of *both* sublimated and sexual activity. The "taming" or "binding" of an instinctual need does not interfere with its satisfaction, but rather makes it possible in both directions. Both functions are able to tolerate delay (metapsychologically speaking, they have come under the sway of secondary process).

Freud (1923) provided the clinical basis for the solution to this enigma at the same time that he formulated the structural theory. He said that the two classes of instinctual drives are "fused, blended and alloyed with each other; . . . that this takes place very regularly and extensively is an assumption indispensable to our conception. . . . We perceive that for purposes of discharge the instinct of destruction is habitually brought into the service of eros" (p. 41).

Anna Freud (1949) continued this theme and added that failure on the part of the environment to provide objects for libidinal satisfaction hampers the process of fusion and leads to the appearance of nonneutralized aggressive tendencies.

As metapsychological speculations (Hartmann, 1955), libido and aggression have been defined as parallel drives capable of independent neutralization and discharge, although optimally operating together. Such isolated manifestations of impulses are not seen, and it contributes nothing but confusion to abandon clinical observation in favor of speculation. It is not possible to describe any psychological phenomena that have the capacity to neutralize aggression that do not manifest a libidinal quality. Likewise, unbridled expressions of destructiveness or sexual sadism regularly demonstrate their roots in frustrations with childhood love objects, and they are recognized to be the result of stresses that jeopardize the normal psychic homeostatic mechanisms; that is, the libidinal components have failed to neutralize the destructiveness of the aggressive drive. It is most likely that the capacity for discharge requires, *as an indispensable precondition*, the fusion of libido and aggression.

It is a paradox that the existence of the aggressive drive is revealed only in response to libidinal frustration. When that occurs, libidinal interests may be taken over by destructive impulses, while libidinal goals retain their infantile qualities. It seems that the libidinal impulses need to be "primed" by infantile gratifications in order to develop their mature qualities, in which case they carry "neutralized" derivatives of the aggressive drives with them.

This is consistent with a statement Freud made in a letter to Marie Bonaparte written in 1937 (quoted in Jones, 1957):

> All activities that rearrange or effect changes are to a certain extent destructive and thus redirect a portion of the instinct from its original destructive goal. Even the sexual instinct, as we know, cannot act without some measure of aggression. Therefore in the regular combination of the two instincts *there is a partial sublimation of the destructive instinct.* [pp. 464–465; italics mine]

These elements can be summarized in the following reconstruction: During the course of psychosexual development there is a component of the aggressive drive that accompanies each libidinal urge. When an infant is frustrated, he manifests an angry response. When gratification becomes available in a reasonable time, the psychic energy that would have expressed itself in the angry response is available to carry out the functions associated with the libidinal urges. The libidinal aspect dominates as a result of its association with gratification, while the aggressive drive becomes subordinated to the libidinal function. The resulting fused drives manifest secondary process qualities with the capacity for delay as a result of the transformation associated with libidinal satisfaction, that is, on the basis of the memory of prior satisfaction.

From a slightly different perspective, the initial gratifications provided by the parents represent *communications* to the infant. The mother communicates empathically with the infant in accordance with both their needs; sublimations, including language, reflect her influence and become the basis for the development of effective communication with others. The "transformation of primary to secondary process" is the metapsychological representation of these events. This correlates with Lorenz's constructions (1963) regarding the "communicative" function of bond behavior.

Blum (1978) has presented a review of the subject of the theoretical differentiation between unconscious primary process symbol formation and secondary process symbolization involved in language, while Loewald (1978) has described secondary process development as an organizing experience mediated by parent-child interaction providing for the development of the sublimated functions of language: "The distinction between sounds and so forth as ingredients of a total occurrence, and what the sounds refer to or signify—this is a slowly developing achievement to which we apply the term secondary process" (pp. 246–247).

The criticism of the concept of the aggressive drive, as recently expressed by Shaw (1978), is answered by these considerations. In his criticism Shaw remarked that

> aggression in man reflects an underlying biological tendency with roots in evolutionary history. . . . Although the neurophysiological mechanisms underlying aggressive behavior are innately determined, the lack of a consensually validated "set goal" and aim toward which aggression is directed would seem to make the concept of aggression as an aggressive instinct virtually meaningless. [p. 51]

If, however, the "set goal" and aim of the aggressive drive parallels libidinal development, the concept of an aggressive drive makes perfectly good sense.

A recent panel on aggression asked a fundamental question, but in the wrong terms: "Does hostile aggression arise inevitably from innate drives genetically or hormonally programmed, or is aggression learned and reactive to frustration, trauma, danger, or other external influences?" (Slap, 1979, p. 655). The question might better be phrased as an inquiry into the *conditions* in which the aggressive drive is *manifested* as either a destructive or a creative force. Genetic roots do not necessarily determine destructiveness, except when mobilized in that direction by specific experiences. The aggressive component of sexual and sublimated activity is not destructive per se, but can readily deteriorate to destructive impulses as a result of frustration.

Neurotic mechanisms of defense operate by means of the intensification or diversion of sublimated operations of the ego. In the analytic setting, interpretations of defense/resistance focus on ego operations that are diverted from their sublimated functions; and they resume those functions if the analysis is successful. For example, Mr. A's predispositions to orderliness and logic were diverted to defending against anxiety associated with infantile conflicts. The resulting compromises inhibited the potential satisfactions associated with their operations. Resolution of the conflict would imply neither the loss of intellectual capacities nor the development of slovenly habits.

Freud (1937), and later Rapaport (1960), raised the question of what maintains "defenses" once they have become established and the conflict underlying them has become quiescent? This issue is no longer a problem. The ego operates primarily by means of sublimated functions. Its operations may become "tainted" by the residues of childhood frustrations or may be "taken over" by these childhood derivatives with resulting neurotic symptoms and behavior. Psychoanalysis restores them, as well as the derivatives of the infantile elements expressed in neurotic conflict, to effective, contemporary operations.

Sublimation and Civilization

Freud's *Civilization and Its Discontents* (1930) continued to reflect the dichotomy between sublimation and sexuality. It is impossible, he wrote there, "to overlook the extent to which civilization is built up upon a renunciation of instinct, how much it presupposes precisely the non-satisfaction (by suppression, repression or some other means?) of powerful instincts" (p. 97). Freud added that "since a man does not have unlimited quantities of psychical energy at his disposal, he has to accomplish his tasks by making an expedient distribution of his libido. What he employs for cultural aims he to a great extent withdraws from women and his sexual life" (pp. 103–104).

Freud was evidently unable to integrate *theoretically* the common experience of pleasurable readiness for work when sex has been satisfying, and conversely, the pleasant anticipation for sexual love when work has gone well. Instead, it would appear that Freud believed that one detracted from the other. This was in contrast, however, to his *clinical* understanding. Jokl (1950) reported personal communications in which Freud explicitly recognized that psychoanalysis resulted in improvement in sexual function as well as in the liberation and strengthening of sublimations.

Since civilization is a product of the efforts of large groups of people, it contains provisions for the reinforcement of defective superego controls with all of their associated unreasonable demands and potentials for violence. It was in this sense that Freud's view of civilization was derived from a description of the frustrations of forbidden oedipal wishes and expressed a renunciation of sexuality as a submission to the oedipal father.

Civilization is both the product of sublimations and the provider of opportunities for sublimated satisfactions. It provides protection against the emergence of destructive impulses by offering multiple pathways for sublimated satisfactions on the widest possible scale. This does not interfere with but enhances the expression and satisfaction of inborn needs.

When neurotic conflicts on a large scale invade the institutions of civilization, the latter become imbued with the rigidity and destructiveness that place them in the service of intraspecific aggression. War and violence do not represent primary biological safeguards or safety valves, but are symptomatic expressions of the failure of the psychological mechanisms that are available to protect against intraspecific aggression. These failures promote biological regressions to derivatives of bond behavior similar to that of the Cichlids, but infinitely more devastating.

While providing a means for the attainment of enormously greater flexibility than the ritualized bonding behavior of other species, the long period of development in man also offers numerous opportunities for failure. Safety valves are available in neurotic symptoms, which are unreliable, as well as in laughter, crying, and dreaming; and when these mechanisms fail, disturbances develop with predispositions to violence which represent unrestrained intraspecific aggression.

Since sublimations are essential for the effective establishment of controls over intraspecific aggression in man, they must represent the biological "norm." They operate most efficiently when associated with the kind of personal relationship expressed by "object constancy," to which they contribute and by means of which they are enhanced. This defines a special reciprocal relationship that contributes to, and provides the means for, the development of like qualities in succeeding generations.

Memories of childhood gratification are essential in order to establish sublimations, and the great memory capacity is likewise an essential element in the diversity of sublimated functions that are available. The ability to remember, however, is countered by the inability to forget, for the significant frustrations of childhood development live on in the unconscious. Man is doomed to repeat unsuccessfully, throughout his lifetime, his efforts to correct those memories through neurotic symptoms, self-defeating character disorders, and, finally, by participation in intraspecific aggression.

Those psychic functions associated with sublimations demonstrate the flexibility, the "free will," of man. Lewy (1961) viewed the confusion surrounding this issue as based on the dichotomy between clinical observations and metapsychological theory. "The findings of psychoanalysis, as of science in general," he wrote, "militate against the assumption of a free choice. This is because psycho-analysis assumes a strictly deterministic view"; he noted also the contrasting theme that the goal of psychoanalysis is "to give the patient's ego freedom to choose one way or the other" (p. 262).

Man's *fixed motor patterns* are more flexible than those of other species, but they are just as dependent upon *releasing mechanisms*. The innate releasing mechanisms become relatively "internalized" in man by means of sublimations, as a consequence of his ability to sustain the image of significant gratifying persons. The reciprocal responses between an individual and the significant persons in his existence, however, are essential to sustain him in his sublimated bond behavior. The gratifying memories in these interactions enlarge both his individuality as well as his creative and empathic capacity, the manifestations of "free will."

When Lorenz (1963) wrote that "a simple effective way of discharging aggression in an innocuous manner is to redirect it at a substitute object" (p. 269), this could not apply to man. In our species the effective means of discharge—of "channeling of aggression into innocuous outlets"—are limited to sublimations and coitus. Otherwise, there is neurosis or hostile aggression. The libidinal gratifications associated with childhood development, along with their reinforcement later in life, create the essential bases for the subordination of the aggressive drive to the libidinal interests. This creates the opportunity for the discharge of aggressive drive derivatives in sublimations as well as sexual activity, while protecting against the deflection of derivatives of the aggressive drive into neurotic symptoms or destructive behavior.

In summary, sublimations can be conceptualized on

three levels. *Clinically*, sublimations describe the range of nonerotic satisfactions and their psychological functions; and they reflect the nonerotic representations of the impulses that are also available for sexual activity. *Metapsychologically*, sublimations describe the range of conflict-free derivatives of psychosexual development that become organized as the ego. *Ethologically*, sublimations describe man's expression of bond behavior, the instinctual functions involved in the displacement and control of intraspecific aggression.

The complexity and sophistication of man's protective devices against intraspecific aggression suggest that a long period of natural selection was necessary to adapt to the potential destructiveness of our species. Whether the destructiveness was initially adaptive or the result of mutation is a moot point. It appears, however, that man's capacity for sublimation is readily diverted to destructive pursuits.

Psychoanalysis has demonstrated that it is not enemies as objects for discharge of aggression, symbolic or otherwise, that we need, but rather persons to love, persons with whom we can interact with sublimated derivatives of the earliest gratifying parent-child relationships. Whether, in the long run, evolution's creation of a species whose instinctual functions require such prolonged periods of development will be a successful experiment, or whether the multitude of failures that we see individually and collectively will culminate in the self-destruction of the species, only time will tell. If psychoanalysis is to provide a positive contribution to this struggle we must define the problems of aggression, with all of their unpleasant and frightening implications, as clearly and objectively as possible.

3

PSYCHIC STRUCTURE AND AFFECTS

The therapeutic and scientific goals of psychoanalysis have a reciprocating relationship which centers on the role of "insight" in the therapeutic process. This involves two clinically related areas of observation and experience, the patient's fantasies and his affects. The former reflect directly the influence of memories involving the significant persons of childhood, along with the distortions and rearrangements that occur during psychic development. The associations of the infantile "imagos" with memories of gratification and frustration determine the quality of their participation in the contemporary pursuit of satisfaction in both sublimated and sexual directions.

Affects are the contemporary driving forces that are associated with memories, and they constitute major elements of the confirmatory data during psychoanalytic investigation. Fantasies are expressions of minor discharges of thought that are associated with the pursuit of satisfaction (Freud, 1911); the affects represent greater discharge phenomena. These psychic constellations are essential for the understanding of the development of the ego, superego, and ego ideal, as well as the related affects of shame, guilt, and depression.

The theory of consciousness has helped to clarify the concept of discharge and to integrate it with clinical concepts. This theory also provides an added dimension for understanding the relationships among psychic structure,

59

psychic representations, and affects. Psychic structure is the result of the development of identifications and the accompanying capacity for sublimations. The integrity of the structural elements and the associated containment of id impulses are reinforced and sustained by the cycle of satisfaction; and secondary controls are sustained by identifications and sublimations as a result of their subordination to defensive functions through pathological character and symptom formations.

Terminology of Psychic Representations

Any theory of the psychic apparatus retains its validity to the extent that its elements correlate with clinical observations; its usefulness is destroyed when these elements are converted into a psychoanalytic mythology. Freud's speculative and philosophical interests may have provided the foundations for such theoretical excursions but did not justify them. Some years ago, Glover (1968) criticized some of the more extreme distortions of metapsychology: "we are now faced with the most elaborate and metaphysical extensions of psycho-analytical 'ego-psychology' which are based not so much on clinical observation as on the ingenuities of armchair thinking [p. 12]."

A review of the literature, however limited, is subject to the pitfalls of confusing and often contradictory definitions of terms. Some of the most important contributors have redefined terms in the context of their individual theoretical biases. Although this may have contributed to the exposition of their theories, it has added to the confusion in psychoanalytic terminology. (See Frosch, 1983, for a recent discussion of this topic.)

Laplanche and Pontalis (1973) have provided coherent definitions based on an historical psychoanalytic perspective. Their definitions provide a useful frame of reference.

Identification: Psychological process whereby the subject assimilates an aspect, property or attribute of the other and is transformed, wholly or partially, after the model the other provides. It is by means of a series of identifications that the personality is constituted and specified. [p. 205]

In their discussion of the development of its meaning, they added,

In Freud's work the concept of identification came little by little to have the central importance which makes it, not simply one psychical mechanism among others, but the operation itself whereby the human subject is constituted. This evolution is correlated chiefly, in the first place, with the coming to the fore of the Oedipus complex viewed in the light of its structural consequences, and secondly, with the revision effected by the second theory of the psychical apparatus, according to which those agencies that become differentiated from the id are given their specific characters by the identifications of which they are the outcome. . . .

The development of the second theory of the psychical apparatus testifies to the new depth and growing significance of the idea of identification. The individual's mental agencies are no longer described in terms of systems in which images, memories and psychical "contents" are inscribed, but rather as the relics (in different modes) of object-relationships. [pp. 206–207]

Introjection: Process revealed by analytic investigation: in phantasy, the subject transposes objects and their inherent qualities from the "outside" to the "inside" of himself.

Introjection is close in meaning to incorporation, which indeed provides it with its bodily model, but it does not necessarily imply any reference to the body's real boundaries (introjection into the ego, into the ego-ideal, etc.).

"It is closely akin to identification." [p. 229]

Laplanche and Pontalis added,

In adopting the term, Freud distinguishes it clearly from projection. His most explicit text on this point is "Instincts and Their Vicissitudes" (1915d), which envisages the genesis of the opposition between subject (ego) and object (outside world) in so far as it can be correlated with that between pleasure and unpleasure: the "purified pleasure-ego" is constituted by an introjection of everything that is a source of pleasure and by the projection outwards of whatever brings about unpleasure. . . .

Introjection is further characterized by its link with oral incorporation; indeed the two expressions are often used synonymously by Freud and many other authors. Freud shows how the antagonism between introjection and projection, before it becomes general, is first expressed concretely in an oral mode. . . . [p. 230]

Incorporation: Process whereby the subject, more or less on the level of phantasy, has an object penetrate his body and keeps it "inside" his body. Incorporation constitutes an instinctual aim and a mode of object-relationship which are characteristic of the oral stage; although it has a special relationship with the mouth and with the ingestion of food, it may also be lived out in relation with other erotogenic zones and other functions. Incorporation provides the corporal model for introjection and identification. [p. 211]

Laplanche and Pontalis added,

Within the framework of his final instinct theory (opposing life to death instincts), it is above all the fusion of libido and aggressiveness that Freud brings to the fore: "During the oral stage of organization of the libido, the act of obtaining erotic mastery over an object coincides with that object's destruction". . . .

Actually incorporation contains three meanings: it means to obtain pleasure by making an object penetrate oneself; it means to destroy this object; and it means, by keeping it within oneself, to appropriate the object's qualities. It is this last aspect that makes incorporation into the matrix of introjection and identification. [p. 212]

Internalization has been appropriated in recent years as a technical term. Laplanche and Pontalis defined it as follows:

a. Term often used as a synonym for "introjection".

b. More specifically, process whereby intersubjective relations are transformed into intrasubjective ones (internalization of a conflict, of a prohibition, etc.). [p. 226]

They added,

In a narrower sense, we only speak of internalisation when it is a *relationship* that is transposed in this way—for example, the relation of authority between father and child is said to be internalised in the relation between super-ego and ego. This process presupposes a structural differentiation within the psyche such that relations and conflicts may be lived out on the intrapsychic level. Such internalisation is correlated with Freud's topographical notions and particularly with his second theory of the psychical apparatus.

Although for reasons of terminological accuracy, we have distinguished two meanings of "internalisation" (a and b above), the two senses are in fact closely linked together: we may say, for instance, that with the decline of the Oedipus complex the subject *introjects* the paternal imago while *internalising* the conflict of authority with the father. [p. 227]

Other authors have approached these topics with varying degrees of consistency. Some definitions of a few of the significant contributors to psychoanalysis will be reviewed in order to illustrate some of the problems. Fenichel (1945) wrote that

> incorporation is the most archaic aim directed at an object. Identification, performed by means of introjection, is the most primitive type of relationship to objects. Therefore, any later type of relationship, upon meeting with difficulties, may regress to identifications, and any later instinctual aim may regress to introjection. [p. 148]

Fenichel's terminology largely reflected Freud's definitions. Hartmann and Loewenstein (1962) held that "there are certainly different kinds of identification. . . . the result of identification is that the identifying person behaves in some ways like the person with whom he has identified himself. . . . We use the term for both the process and the result" (p. 49). They added, "Incorporation we call an instinctual activity, belonging primarily to the oral phase. It is considered a genetic precursor of identification; and the latter is formed after its model" (p. 49). They did not attempt a differentiation of incorporation and introjection and said, "The uncertainties of definition seem to be particularly marked in the use of the term introjection" (p. 51).

Hartmann and Loewenstein also defined the broader concept of internalization:

> We would speak of *internalization* when regulations that have taken place in interaction with the outside world are replaced by internal regulations. The development through which trial activities in the outside world are gradually replaced by thought processes is an example of what we have in mind. [p. 48]

Internalization referred to a broad spectrum of interactions between the self and the outside world, including complex ego-developmental processes. The proposed concept of internalization appears to be logical, as long as it is understood in a purely descriptive, rather than explanatory sense.

Loewald (1962) also emphasized internalization as a major psychological process. However, he extended the definition proposed by Hartmann and Loewenstein:

> I use the term "internalization" here as a general term for certain processes of transformation by which relationships and interactions between the individual psychic apparatus and its environment are changed into inner relationships and interactions with the outer world. The term "internalization" therefore covers such "mechanisms" as incorporation, introjection, and identification, or those referred to by the terms "internal object" and "internalized object," as well as such "vicissitudes of instincts" as the "turning inward" of libidinal and aggressive drives. The word "incorporation" most often seems to emphasize zonal, particularly oral, aspects of internalization processes. "Introjection" ordinarily is used for ego aspects of the same process. "Identification" probably is the term that is most ambiguous. There are reasons to assume that internalization per se is only one element of at least certain kinds of identification and that projection plays an important part in them. The term "identification," in accordance with general psychoanalytic parlance, is used here in a somewhat loose fashion so as not to prejudge what might be implied in the concept. [p. 489]

In the development of his thesis regarding ego and superego development, Loewald went on to add an additional metaphor: "If we think in such terms as 'degrees of internalization,' of greater or lesser 'distance from an ego core,' it is of great importance to keep in mind that the modification of external material for introjection, brought about by internalization, varies with the degree of internalization" (p. 498). Loewald has offered some valuable contributions for viewing ego development, but his ideas are obscured by confusing terminology.

Sandler and Rosenblatt (1962) suggested,

> Identification becomes for us a modification of the self-representation on the basis of another (usually an object) representation as a model. . . . Within the representational world of the child, identification with an object would be the coalescence or fusion of a self-representation and an object representation, or a change in the self-representation so that the object representation is duplicated. . . .
>
> Introjection, as we have defined it (we refer here to the introjections which normally accompany the resolution of the Oedipus complex, and which result in the formation of a structural superego), would be a completely different process. It can be regarded as the vesting of certain object representations with a special status, so that these are felt to have all the authority and power of the real parents. . . . Introjection in this sense means that the child reacts, in the absence of the parents, as if they were present. It does not mean that the child copies the parents—this would be identification. [pp. 137–138]

Sandler and Rosenblatt emphasized the "self-representation" in their description of "identification," while "introjection" was applied to the development of the superego.

Beres (1966) approached the problem of definitions somewhat differently:

> Identification is an essential process for the establishment of internalization, but identification is not the same as

internalization. . . . Identification precedes internalization. . . .

We recognize in human activity, in children as well
as adults, the response to perceptual stimuli by which
what was in the external world is represented in the
mind, in the internal world that Freud speaks of. The
analogy to the instinctual process of "taking in" leads us
to name the process *incorporation*. The capacity of the
human mind to create symbols transforms the incorporated perception into mental representations, what Freud
called "Vorstellung". . . . Incorporation may be expressed as a fantasy of *introjection*, and the product of
this fantasy is the *introject*. . . .

As the child takes on the attributes of the incorporated object, we recognize the process of identification. . . .

The final step in this process is *internalization*, when
the attributes of the object with which the child has identified become his own. [pp. 488–490]

Beres's differentiation of "incorporation" and "introjection" is not clear, and it appears that he may reverse Fenichel's definitions. "Identification" is not defined as a
primitive relationship to an object. "Internalization" differs
considerably from its use by Hartmann and Loewenstein,
in that its use does not apply strictly to "regulations." Also,
Beres uses "internalization" where Sandler and Rosenblatt
would use "identification."

Schafer (1968) at first adopted the definition of internalization suggested by Hartmann and Loewenstein, adding that "it is nevertheless consistent with the developmental
point of view to term the higher-order forms of restraint,
guidance and mastery 'the regulations' " (p. 11). He added,
"Hitherto, introjection has been used by many authors,
often by Freud, to refer to those processes that interiorize
previously external regulations. It is proposed here, however, that internalization is the better rubric for these proc-

esses" (p. 16). Instead, he suggested that "an introject is an inner presence with which one feels in a continuous or intermittent dynamic relationship. . . . Both the coming into being of an introject and its continued existence represent attempts to modify distressing relationships with the external object" (pp. 72–73). Schafer also suggested that

> identification is sharply distinguished from introjection. Introjection. . . . does not aim at likeness, sameness, or merging: it aims to continue a relation with an object, but to displace this relation from the outer world to the inner world; the object is preserved, though perhaps transformed, in the inner world. In contrast, identification aims to transform the self along the lines of the object; the object is implied in the identification, and is thus carried into the inner world too, but not as an altogether separate object. [pp. 153–154]

These definitions appear somewhat similar to the use of "introjection" and "identification" by Sandler and Rosenblatt. They, as well as Schafer, sacrificed the use of "introjection" as an instinctual process. Schafer did this in order to provide a term for what might be termed descriptively an ambivalent object representation, while Sandler and Rosenblatt similarly emphasized its special status in the superego. Later, Schafer (1976) revised his definitions in his effort to replace Freud's metapsychology with his own "action language":

> When we use the term internalization, we refer not to a fantasy but to a psychological process, and we are saying that a shift of event, action, or situation in an inward direction or to an inner locale has occurred. For example, a boy imposes on himself prohibitions hitherto imposed on him by his parents: we think of internality or insideness as having more or less replaced outsideness. [p. 155]

. . . from these considerations . . . introjection can only be a synonym of incorporation, which is to say that it must refer to the fantasy of taking something into one's body. In this light it is redundant without appearing to be so, and if kept in use can only be confusing. [p. 160]

. . . we are able to speak about identification as a change in the way one conceives of oneself and perhaps a corresponding change in the way one behaves publicly; as before, the change would be modeled on personal and unconsciously elaborated versions of significant figures in real life or imaginative life. [p. 161]

Jacobson (1964) defined the terms in her reconstructions of early childhood development, and I think that this made her thesis less difficult to understand, although she could not avoid the danger always inherent in any reconstruction of preverbal phenomena.

Thus the hungry infant's longing for food, libidinal gratifications, and physical merging with the mother, which is the precursor of future object-relations, is also the origin of the first, primitive type of identification, identification achieved by refusion of self and object images. . . . [p. 40]

To begin with, the terms introjection and projection refer to psychic processes, as a result of which self images assume characteristics of object images and vice versa. The mechanisms of introjection and projection originate in infantile incorporation and ejection fantasies and must be distinguished from them. They undergo elaborate vicissitudes, may be employed in the service of defense, and in psychotics are used for restitution. . . . [p. 46]

The small child's limited capacity to distinguish between the external and internal world, which is responsible for the weakness of the boundaries between self and object and the drastic cathectic shifts between them, promotes continuous operation of projective and introjective

processes. Thus, it is quite true that during the first years
of life the self and object images have more or less introjective and projective qualities. . . . [p. 47]

As these [infantile] trends develop, the child's desire
to remain part of his love objects, or to make them part
of his own self will slowly recede and give way to wishes
for realistic likeness with them. This goal can be achieved
by virtue of selective identifications, based on mechanisms of "partial introjection". . . . [p. 50]

We can also observe identification which, developing
directly from the child's close intimacy with his love object, remains centered about it and hardly acquires any
reactive or defensive qualities. . . .

Quite a different variety of identifications originates
in the child's indomitable competitive urges for sexual
gratification and narcissistic expansion. They induce
wishful fantasies of sexual identification with aggran-
dized images of his love objects, predominantly of his
admired preoedipal and oedipal rivals. Such familiar fantasies acquire increasingly aggressive qualities to the extent to which the child rebels against the instinctual
frustration and narcissistic injuries and wants to break
his symbiotic ties with his parents. [p. 90]

Meissner (1980) opted for a somewhat different approach that required the concept of self as a primary metapsychological concept.

The problem of internalization, then, arises at that
point at which properties and characteristics of the external object that have been translated and intended as
part of the object-representation are then further proc-
essed so that they become an inherent part of the organization of the subject's self. [p. 240]

In his discussion of incorporation, Meissner said,

In regard to incorporation, it is difficult to know what

to say. . . . There are no reasonable grounds on which we can presume the effective operations of a separate psychic agency such as the ego from earliest infancy. . . .

The process of introjection operates . . . so that we can say that the process terminates in a modification of the self-system. . . . The self-organization or introject may have varying degrees of structuralization and differentiation in itself. It may serve as a discrete and persistent focus of relatively dissociated psychic activity, as in the case of the pathological superego, or it may function in less discrete and more diffuse ways and may even be integrated with aspects of the organization of the ego. . . .

Identification takes place in the context of mature object-relations, and functions more in terms of the relatively autonomous and adaptive aspects of ego functioning, rather than defensive. . . .

Identification is, therefore, an active structuralizing process taking place within the ego; it is the process by which the ego constructs the inner constituents of regulatory control on the basis of selective elements derived from object-relations. [pp. 242–243]

Meissner defined "identification" where others have used "internalization," that is, in terms of the development of ego functions, the "regulations." To him, the self-representational aspects reflecting the imago of the parent is not a part of this process. Rather, this is included in his discussion of internalization. He uses introjection as a complex term in order to complete his description of the development of his theory of the self, about which he says, "The view of the self that I am proposing here would see the self as an epiphenomenal or intersystemic organization which would include all of the psychic agencies in a superordinate integration" (p. 241).

I will not add a review of the vicissitudes of the term "self," which has in recent years developed its own maze of semantic confusion. Rangell (1982) and Blum (1982), among others, have recently elaborated on this issue. Meissner as well as other authors who have attempted to provide it metapsychological status have been unable to provide a definition they are comfortable with. In common usage the term refers to *subjective* phenomena, and its application to metapsychology is questionable.

The student of psychoanalysis has the burden of correlating the use of terms by different authors while he attempts to understand the concepts and to integrate them with clinical observations. A close relationship of psychoanalytic theory with clinical observation needs to be reemphasized, while an historical perspective in the application of psychoanalytic concepts is maintained as much as is possible.

Psychic Structure

Freud's discussion of diverse psychological processes under the rubric of identification undoubtedly contributed to the confusion in terminology. This was typified in "The New Introductory Lectures on Psycho-Analysis" (1933):

> I cannot tell you as much as I should like about the metamorphosis of the parental relationship into the super-ego, partly because . . . we ourselves do not feel sure that we understand it completely. . . .
> The basis of the process is what is called an "identification"—that is to say, the assimilation of one ego to another one, as a result of which the first ego behaves like the second in certain respects, imitates it and in a sense takes it up into itself. Identification has been not unsuitably compared with the oral, cannibalistic incorporation of the other person. It is a very important form of attachment to someone else, probably the very first, and not the same thing as the choice of an object. The

difference between the two can be expressed in some such way as this. If a boy identifies himself with his father, he wants to be like his father; if he makes him the object of his choice, he wants to *have* him, to possess him. In the first case his ego is altered on the model of his father; in the second case that is not necessary. Identification and object-choice are to a large extent independent of each other; it is however possible to identify oneself with someone whom, for instance, one has taken as a sexual object, and to alter one's ego on his model. . . . If one has lost an object or has been obliged to give it up, one often compensates oneself by identifying oneself with it and by setting it up once more in one's ego, so that here object-choice regresses, as it were, to identification. [p. 63]

Freud included in "identification" psychological processes of "assimilation" of one ego by another, imitation, fantasies of incorporation, a primitive kind of "attachment," and a "compensatory" mechanism related to object loss. The relationships between object-choice and identification also remained obscure. He asserted that identification "is a very important form of attachment to someone else," but "not the same thing as a choice of an object," and "identification and object choice are to a large extent independent of each other." "Incorporative" fantasies participated in "identification," while "choice of an object" involved the fantasy "to have," or "possess," the object, which also suggests a fantasy of incorporation.

To bring some order into this highly complex subject, it might help to summarize the various functions and roles of psychic representations in the psychic economy. First, the development of ego functions that result from the earliest interactions between infant and parent are related to the earliest psychic representations. These ego functions, including those associated with object investments and object constancy, evolve parallel to the establishment of the parental imago as a source of gratifications. Second, the self-image and the rudiments of self-esteem are modified according to perceptions of these interactions.

Third, less integrated psychic representations are manifested in functions associated with the superego. These imagos have a sense of separateness in the operations of the mind, although they may become confused between the areas "internal" and "external" to the self. Some authors have referred to these as "introjects." The "projected" psychic representations that are extruded from the ego, but are manifestations of fantasies of diverse origins, may be considered a related subgroup. They reflect problems associated with self-object differentiation, and they may become the basis of further psychological developments.

Those transference representations observed during analytic treatment, those that are associated with the neurotic compulsion to repeat, must also be recognized as an overlapping, but separate group. They reflect the demands for the continuation of relationships with retained childhood "imagos," or psychic representations, in the analytic setting.

Confusion regarding reconstructions of early structure formation can be minimized if they are derived from and consistent with observations. In a purely descriptive sense, identifications may be primary or secondary. That is, those identifications occurring before there is a stable ego are divided from those taking place after its establishment. The two stages are, of course, broadly overlapping. (Loewald [1962] also separated primary and secondary identifications according to pre-superego and superego stages.)

The earliest manifestations of libidinal needs provide the conditions for the psychological investments of gratifying objects. The psychic representation of the gratifying object is stabilized as a result of repeated satisfactions. The ego functions that emerge include the recognition of the external object as a potential source of gratification. The result is that necessary attachments begin, while the precarious self-object boundaries are stabilized. The repeated gratifications also influence the development of the rudiments of self-esteem.

We may be justified in applying the term "identification" for this process as long as we acknowledge the limitations of this concept at such an early developmental stage. The rudiments of object-love are established in response to the loving parent; but this is distinct from an imitation of, or an alteration of, the self-representation in the image of the mother. The one-year-old infant, for example, cannot experience object-love in a manner similar to, that is, in imitation of, his mother's. The experiences of satisfaction contribute to the flexibility of the ego's operations appropriate to the given stage of development, rather than to an image of the parent that is copied.

Continuing satisfactions lead, in turn, to the stabilization of the associated ego functions. The stability of the corresponding "ego nucleus" is based on confidence in the future availability of satisfactions from the object, along with the foundations for the capacity to pursue emotional investments in new objects. Qualities of the earliest satisfactions undoubtedly contain the rudiments of later object investments.

Glover's (1968) description of "ego nuclei" is a convenient concept that helps reconstruct the development of the ego. The concept permits the useful formulation that "ego nuclei" are "memory substructures" that may undergo continuing modifications as a consequence of subsequent gratifications and frustrations. This is consistent with clinical observations of modifications of earlier substructures, in contrast to the repetitious quality of neurotic mechanisms.

The ego nuclei evidently represent the precursors of stable identifications that constitute the ego. In the latter sense the *integration* of the ego means that the specific ego functions do not require the persistence of the parental imago. This does not imply repression, but refers to the relinquishment of the dependence on the parental imago for the pursuit of satisfaction. This provides a definition of psychic structure as a stable psychic constellation associated with memories of satisfaction and sustained by further satisfactions. It implies that the libidinal and aggressive drives operate in a synergistic mode toward mature satisfactions, that is, that they are also integrated. Those functions that require the persistence of the parental imago, even when repressed, reflect a lesser degree of integration and a less stable structure.

Loewald (1973) described the integrative processes somewhat differently, while emphasizing superego development. "Repression," he wrote,

> tends to keep object representations and object relations on an infantile level. Internalization, on the other hand, is a process by which, in the example of superego formation, oedipal object relations are renounced as such, destroyed, and the resulting elements enter into the formation of higher psychic structure, leading in turn to the development of object relations of a higher order of organization. [p. 12]

The relationship between identification and object choice also needs to be more clearly defined. Beginning with Freud, an artificial dichotomy has been established between these psychic functions. This was based on an *assumption*, one that has been sustained by theory, not by observation. Empathy, the kind of transient identification that is necessary for successful object relations in the adult, combines object-investment with fusion fantasies. It is reasonable to speculate that the earliest emotional investments of the infant that are associated with satisfaction include fantasies of merging with the object. Such normal satisfactions could not jeopardize self-object boundaries, and they undoubtedly contribute to stabilizing those boundaries.

The complex psychological processes that represent mature emotional investments are demonstrated by patients well along in analysis. Only when the patient achieves a significant degree of nonambivalent investment in the analyst that is manifested by a (symbolic) level of sleep and merging with the analyst is the therapeutic process—and the significant modification of the ego—most effective (see chapter 6). This quality of emotional investment is not unique to the analytic setting. The resolution of the associated conflicts during analytic treatment leads to its intensification, but the quality of response is not idiosyncratic to analysis.

All emotional investments, to the extent that they are free of conflict, include a quality of merging which is often described as a transient (empathic) identification with the object. To say that this represents a narcissistic investment is tautologous, however accurate it might be. In the absence of this quality, regardless of which terms we choose to describe it, satisfaction is lacking, and neurotic conflicts are regularly observed to intrude on the process. Borderline and psychotic patients may sometimes be able to translate behavior for defensive purposes, but they have limited capacity for empathy due to its association with unconscious fantasies of incorporation and destruction.

No primary confusion of self and object needs to be hypothesized according to this construction, although the primitive ego's intolerance of frustration creates a precarious relationship with external reality.

It is almost axiomatic to many analysts that the foundations of the ego establish self-object boundaries, and that these functions derive primarily from the earliest experiences of the infant. It has been convenient to conclude that the ego boundaries emerge from an earlier narcissistic matrix in which self and object are undifferentiated. It might equally be possible to conceptualize that self and object, that is, inside and outside, are primarily not undifferentiated; and that any subsequent dedifferentiation results from an effort to reject, to destroy in fantasy, that which is a potential source of frustration. Disruption of self-object differentiation is a major pathological event, but it does not necessarily demonstrate regression to an earlier "normal" state.

M. Klein (1981) has reviewed studies of infantile behavior that suggest a primary sense of intrapsychic separateness of self and object, and also that the infant appears to seek and to need stimuli. He concluded, "The infant is highly differentiated and begins to differentiate objects from day one" (p. 102). Although the same limitations regarding reconstructions of preverbal phenomena must apply to my efforts, Klein's conclusions derived from infant observations coincide with my speculations based on psychoanalytic inferences. The "cycle of satisfaction" expresses the essential stimulus-seeking quality of adult behavior, and there is evidence that this is a biological characteristic from the time of birth.

The later identifications can be further subdivided into those associated principally with gratifications, and those associated with frustrating experiences. Those secondary identifications resulting from frustrations necessarily involve responses to a loved object and result in ambivalent object representations. The importance of the love object plus the immaturity of the ego results in an alteration of the ego, with the result that there is a split within the ego which reflects the ambivalence. The submission to the split-off representation is ambivalent and is associated with the projected or perceived hatred of the loved person.

When a child loves, he becomes what he loves. He is also able to take over the guilt for his parents in order to protect them from his hatred, and himself from his ambivalence. He thereby sustains the image of a loving parent whom he can love in return. This contributes to his feeling "real," or "whole," while it supports the flexibility of the ego to pursue satisfaction within the limits of the superego prohibitions.

The ambivalent identifications of the superego become relatively organized and function to ward off "danger." In its response to such fantasied dangers, it operates like a neurotic symptom, with repressed hostile impulses displaced onto the self. That is, the establishment of an ambivalent identification represents a response to unresolved conflict with compromise formations. In the superego its function is to ward off, or defend principally against the residues of oedipal conflict. While there may be relatively successful defenses, the infantile qualities of the superego are particularly manifested in its orientation toward revenge and punishment. (Sandler and Rosenblatt [1962], as well as others, have noted the connection of the superego with unresolved conflict.)

The superego identifications represent only one distinct group of secondary identifications. Fantasied fusions with a love-object may occur well after the establishment of the superego. They provide the bases for additional ego identifications and alterations of character throughout life, unless there is an impairment in the capacity for gratifying object relations. The younger and more immature the individual, the greater is this tendency. However, after the stabilization of the ego, those identifications associated with satisfaction contribute to the development of normal character traits and reinforce specific directions for sublimations. They also tend to reinforce the earliest primary identifications.

Sublimations have their roots in the preoedipal stages of development, and they are modified and reinforced by the identifications associated with the Oedipus complex. When the emotional climate is predominantly and appropriately gratifying to the child, realistic and gratifying ideals are established in identification with the parents. I think that the term "ego ideal" is most appropriate to this situation. The corresponding moral convictions, or ideals, likewise differ on the bases of whether they derive from gratifying experiences or from ambivalent identifications. Those based on unresolved conflict—I would say on superego identifications—reflect this conflict in their unreliability. The identifications with the father in the *resolution* of the Oedipus complex implies a submission to the father who is loved. To the extent that childhood development makes this possible, the infantile attachment to the mother can be abandoned and its derivatives, along with the loving attachment to the father, can be mobilized to develop moral convictions and sublimations based on positive concern for others.

In a similar vein, Loewald (1962) wrote,

> The changing of superego elements into ego elements involves a further desexualization and deaggressivization; it involves a return, as in a spiral, to the type of identifications characterized as ego or primary identifications—regaining a measure of narcissistic wholeness which inevitably, as in childhood, leads again to loss of such self-sufficiency by further involvement with others. [p. 500]

This perspective also helps to describe the identifications that evolve during the course of analysis. The terminology of "identification" has been used in different contexts in regard to psychoanalytic technique. Glover (1955) said, "And we must be able to recognize when an ego defense [as identification] is pursuing its normal course and when it is being used as a protection against analysis itself" (p. 64).

The neurotic transferences observed during psychoanalytic treatment derive from "ambivalent representations." The ambivalence prevents the integration of the infantile needs associated with the imagos such that the past can be forgotten rather than reexperienced. The defensive manifestation of "identification" is observed in the analytic situation in the patient's imitation of the analyst. I would prefer not to use the term in this context, "imitation" probably conveying a more accurate description. This manifestation of resistance often reflects an idealization of the analyst that defends against anxiety associated with negative transference; while "identification" might be limited to more or less successful integrative experiences of the ego.

In its "healing function," separation from the analyst requires the *integration* of the analyst's image, just as normal development requires the integration of the parental imagos. This is a significant feature that differentiates psychoanalysis from psychoanalytic psychotherapy. It defines the circumstances whereby "id is replaced by ego." In contrast, psychoanalytic psychotherapy may provide insight into infantile conflicts and their derivatives so that the conflicts may be dealt with more rationally. It does not replace ambivalent identifications, nor does it resolve the dependence on the therapist.

In this thesis, "identification," "integration," "sublimation," and "ambivalent identification" are terms whose primary referents are clinical, and they are valid and useful to the extent that their relationships with clinical data are maintained. "Identification" expresses the effects of the significant psychic representations on the organization and structuralization of the id into the ego. The intensity of the ambivalence negatively influences the degree of integration. To the extent that there is an integrative experience the psychic structure becomes relatively free of the parental imago, even as the parental attachment evolves along its normal course of development; while the imago persists in the residual ambivalent structures. "Sublimation" describes the ego functions associated with well-integrated representations.

The ego of the adult represents the psychic derivatives of infantile and childhood gratifications. It defines the mature psychological processes that are involved in the pursuit of both sublimated and sexual satisfactions. Those ego functions that are invaded by the effects of excessive infantile frustrations and ambivalent imagos become involved in defensive operations and neurotic compromises.

Affects

The "integration of object representations into the ego" defines, in metapsychological perspective, the essential condition for the pursuit of satisfaction. The ego develops from the instinctual drives of the id as a result of satisfaction, and its functional "integrity" is sustained by the cycle of satisfaction. The instinctual drives impose a constant demand for renewals of the satisfactions, with a constant threat of deterioration of the ego's capacities following excessive frustration. Affects reflect the struggle between the pursuit of satisfaction and adaptations to its absence.

The thesis that there is a consistent relationship between pleasure and discharge, and between tension and psychic pain, provides an important foundation for a description and classification of affects. Affects express manifestations of the "drives," or psychological "needs," that accompany psychic "content" or fantasies. Freud (1915b) described this dichotomy: "Quota of affect corresponds to the instinct insofar as the latter has become detached from the idea and finds expression, proportionate to its quantity, in processes which are sensed as affects" (p. 152).

It is a paradox that satisfaction, or "pleasure," is poorly defined and documented. Major aspects of the ego are separated from their infantile roots as a consequence of the integrative experiences of growth and development, with the result that they are outside the purview of psychoanalytic investigation. Those affects associated with memories of frustration, the tension affects, retain the ambivalent psychic representations from the past, a fact that makes them amenable to investigation in the transference neuroses.

Glover (1938) described some of the problems of a classification of affects: "affective phenomena," he wrote,

> call for a greater variety of approaches than any other mental manifestation. This is born out by the fact that affects can be classified in a great variety of ways. They can be described in crude, qualitative terms, e.g. of subjective pleasure or "pain," or labelled descriptively according to the predominant ideational system associated with them in consciousness. They can be classified by the reference to the instinct or component instinct from which they are derived, or they can be considered as either "fixed" or "labile." They can be divided into primary affects or secondary affects, more precisely into "positive" or "reactive" affects, or they can be considered as tension and discharge phenomena. Finally, they can be grouped as simple or compound ("mixed" and/or "fused") affects. [p. 299]

Glover added that "the most useful classification of affects seems to be that into tension affects and discharge affects" (p. 301). Glover's classification was limited, however, due to his belief that "there is no exact correlation between tension and 'pain,' or between discharge and 'pleasure' " (p. 302).

Jacobson (1953) proposed a classification of affects within the framework of the structural theory. She said:

> Even though all affects are ego experiences and develop in the ego, one of their qualitative determinants must be the site of the underlying tension by which they have been induced and which may arise anywhere within the psychic organization. . . .
>
> My suggestion for classification is to distinguish: (1) simple and compound affects arising from intrasystemic tension: (a) affects that represent instinctual drives proper; i.e., that arise directly from tension in the id (e.g., sexual excitement, rage); (b) affects that develop directly from tensions in the ego (e.g., fear of reality and physical pain as well as components of the more enduring feelings and feeling attitudes, such as object love and hate or thing interest); (2) simple and compound affects induced by intersystemic tensions: (a) affects induced by tensions between the ego and the id (e.g., fear of the id, components of disgust, shame and pity); (b) affects induced by tensions between ego and superego [e.g., guilt feelings, components of depression]. [p. 46]

Brenner (1974) also proposed a unified theory of affects. He said in his summary:

> 1. Affects are complex mental phenomena which include (a) sensations of pleasure, unpleasure, or both, and (b) ideas. Ideas and pleasure/unpleasure sensations together constitute an affect as a mental or psychological phenomena.

2. The development of affects and their differentiation from one another depend on ego and, later, superego development. Indeed the development and differentiation of affects is an important aspect of ego development.

3. Affects have their beginning early in life when ideas first become associated with sensations of pleasure and unpleasure. Such sensations are most frequently and most importantly associated with drive tension (lack of gratification) and drive discharge (gratification). They constitute the undifferentiated matrix from which the entire gamut of the affects of later life develop. [p. 554]

Rangell (1974) described "the multiple functions of affects: as expressions (of internal forces), as communication (to external objects), as signal (mainly internal, but also external), and as symptom" (p. 612).

Within these frames of reference, affects can be divided into two groups, those associated with gratification (pleasure) and those with frustration (unpleasure). The former are further subdivided into erotic and sublimated pleasurable affects.

Frustration affects can also be divided into two classes, those associated with the direct effects of frustration, such as anger and grief; and those that are available as anticipatory signals, such as anxiety, shame, and guilt. The signal group of affects may be classified and described primarily according to the levels of ego development which they reflect, and secondly by the fantasies associated with their libidinal stages.

The instinctual elements in affects are described metapsychologically by three states: neutralized drives which reflect their integration into the ego and are manifested by object-love, affection, and pleasure; nonneutralized aggression manifested by hostile affects; and nonneutralized libidinal drives with fantasies associated with somatic sources. The latter two are associated with psychic pain, and they intrude upon the operations of the neutralized drives. Anxiety, shame, and guilt may imply anticipation and provide a homeostatic function for the containment of nonneutralized drives.

The earliest representation of an "object" is the result of satisfaction, so that the earliest manifestation of hostility that is able to reach consciousness is ambivalence. Before a libidinal attachment is established, the infant's responses to frustration are probably complex physiological reflexes rather than nonspecific responses by an as yet unformed psychic apparatus (see also Wallace, 1975; Schur, 1955). The tension affects represent the vicissitudes of the ego's efforts to cope with residual ambivalence.

Freud's later theory of anxiety (1926) provided important genetic and object-relations perspectives. Rangell (1968a) has provided an excellent review of anxiety as a tension affect.

The affects shame and guilt provide a particularly difficult problem because they are subjectively so difficult to differentiate and because of their tendency to overlap in so many situations. In an earlier work I suggested that "the difference is that shame is involved in seeking libidinal supplies from an external person, while in guilt the relationship is to the introjected person (superego)" (1963, p. 85). Beres (1966) agreed, stating that guilt differs from shame, "in that the former stems from internalized conflict and the latter with conflict with an external authority" (p. 487).

The most significant differentiating factor involved in the genesis of shame and guilt appears to be the relative maturity of the ego. The superego-conscience evolves after ego development has permitted the child to observe that his parents have an attachment to each other that interferes with his wishes, and to begin the oedipal struggle within a triangular love situation. Shame is related more to conflicts surrounding earlier diadic relationships. The danger includes primitive cannibalistic fantasies, and the underlying wish to be loved is experienced as a wish to merge. Rangell (1954) traced

> the following sequence and line of development: (1) Infant with its mouth and snout buried in the breast. (2) 1½-year-old in its mother's arms, when approached by a stranger, turning and burrowing into his mother's shoulder. (3) Older child turning its face into a corner so as not to be seen, and (4) Adult, unpoised, blushing, and wanting to cover or hide his face. [p. 325]

With shame the genetic conflicts may be repeated in the transference as with guilt, the difference being that the roots of the anxiety are more primitive. The two affective responses are developmentally separate and manifest differing levels of ego integration. Patients with intense shame responses often present as "narcissistic" patients with extremely punitive superegos, but issues related to shame may be more prominent than guilt. Human contact is essential to these patients in order to feel "alive," or "real," but primitive fantasies associated with the "oral triad" interfere. The intolerance of a third person does not necessarily imply oedipal conflict, but may reveal a demand for a regressive diadic relationship. If the frightening merger fantasies are associated with regressive efforts to cope with threatened object-loss rather than expressions of a primary ego deficit, analysis may be possible.

Brenner (1974) noted that " 'affects' must be analyzed just like other mental phenomena, such as neurotic symptoms, dreams, fantasies and the like" (p. 546). Anthony (1981) emphasized the analysis of paranoid elements associated with shame.

When we consider the total shame response, including

the exhibitionistic element that is associated with merger fantasies, the projective mechanisms, the anxiety regarding loss of love, along with the sense of helplessness and the self-debasing attitude associated with the intensely dependent needs, we observe much more than a simple affective experience. Instead there is a complex defensive formation similar to that associated with the superego, with preoedipal manifestations of oral and anal conflicts, and with its primary roots involved in the struggle to maintain object relationships. The resolution of shame-related conflicts involves the establishment of pride and the pursuit of self-esteem. In that sense the affect of shame can provide an intrapsychic stimulus for the pursuit of sublimated satisfactions.

Shame also participates in oedipal conflict. Freud emphasized the association of shame with the fantasied deficiencies of females (1933, p. 132). My own clinical observations indicate that the affect is significant in both genders, however. It is associated with feelings of dependency, helplessness, inferiority, and envy that result from early maternal frustrations and defensive formations associated with the oral triad. Shame is a response not only to ambivalence related to the inability to possess the mother, but also to dependent feelings associated with the pleasures that she provides. "Breast envy" develops early in both genders, and in females the shame syndrome is reinforced by the conflicts associated with the emergence of the positive oedipal stage. Among male patients, it is difficult to abandon the masculine ("macho") reaction formations that defend against the shame of their helpless dependent feelings toward women.

Castration fear in the male is not only a reaction to the fear of father's retaliation for the wish to possess the mother. The sexual impulses toward the mother provide in fantasy the means for domination of the mother and retaliation for the shame experienced at her hands. Retaliation is feared from both the mother and the father.

Both shame and envy are parallel affective responses to frustration from a loved person. They predispose to paranoid responses in both genders. There is a greater literature regarding shame in women, but I am not convinced that it represents a more difficult problem for them than for men. Women are able to overcome many of their early frustrations at the hands of the mother by means of secondary identifications with her, and especially by childbearing. Men's envy of women and associated shame does not permit that solution.

The roots of the superego derive from the idealized image of the father and contribute to the idealization of the self. They are associated with moral convictions and defend against destructive fantasies (Freud, 1923). The superego also has roots in preoedipal conflicts, which, with the ambivalent quality of superego imagos, predispose to regressions to shame. The back and forth movements of shame and guilt and their varying combinations provide a major clinical challenge in all patients.

Shame and guilt are complex affects that are available for signal functions, which implies that they also function as motives for defense (e.g., Fenichel, 1945). In guilt, there is the threat of loss of love from an incompletely integrated object representation; in shame, the object representation is also ambivalent, but its precursors reside in earlier stages of development.

Depression is a pathological affect that also describes a vicissitude of ambivalence. It expresses a prolongation of grief when the normal process of mourning fails. Both grief and depression represent reactions to object-loss. Mourning is the process by which the representation of the lost object is reintegrated into the ego in a manner such that the ego's homeostasis becomes independent of the external object.

The following reconstructions will answer the metapsychological question raised by Freud (1917) regarding the process of mourning: "Why this compromise by which the command of reality is carried out piecemeal should be so extra-ordinarily painful is not at all easy to explain in terms of economics" (p. 245). The two elements in grief and mourning that must be considered are the experience of pain and the reparative nature of the process which leads to a resolution of the pain.

Grief is initiated by the loss of a highly cathected love object. Since we are dealing with an intrapsychic process it is necessary to describe what is meant by a "lost" object. This needs to be examined from the perspective of the "cycle of satisfaction." That is, there is ordinarily a reciprocal relationship between an internal object representation and the external object that it represents. A state of relative "harmony" is sustained by repeated satisfactions from the external object. In this context, the "economic function" of the external object is to maintain the stability of the ego functions that are associated with its psychic representations. The original, intense emotional investment of the object was stimulated by satisfactions in the relationship, and the continued stability of the ego depends upon repetitions of the satisfactions. The affective experience of love undoubtedly provides the most significant discharge into consciousness that is available to maintain psychic homeostasis and the neutralized state of the drives.

The pain in grief is the expression of the frustration, of the buildup of instinctual need that has become associated with the lost object. This stimulates a tendency toward deneutralization of the drives that are attached to the lost object and the emergence of ambivalence, just as obtains following any frustration. The hostility may provoke guilt, but that is not the primary element in grief. In order for the psychic pain and ambivalence to be resolved by the process of mourning, the object representation and its associated drives must become relatively independent of the external object, so that the individual can seek gratification elsewhere. (As Freud observed, it is doubtful that the work of mourning is ever completely and finally accomplished.)

Mourning can be compared with the process of working through in psychoanalysis, where the patient is helped to relinquish his attachment to the childhood imagos involved in his neurotic conflicts. The residual ambivalence prevents the patient from abandoning the childhood imagos prior to analysis. When the patient reexperiences the childhood traumas in the transference neurosis the analyst becomes the frustrating person, the representation of the ambivalent imago. His interpretations then restore the image of the analyst as a *gratifying* person. The result is that the patient experiences a loss of the childhood imago, which must be mourned. The libidinal attachments to the childhood imagos which have become freed by the interpretations, along with the basic positive transference, provide the supportive structure, the sublimated gratifications that are essential for the completion of this mourning process. (This is discussed at greater length in subsequent chapters.)

Likewise, grief is a consequence of the attachment to the representation of the lost object. In dynamic-economic terms, the fond memories of the loved person are mobilized repeatedly for discharge into consciousness. The grieving person maintains the relationship with the absent person in fantasy. Mourning, then, is a period of enforced day dreaming. If the lost object is "forgotten" for a while, the recurrence of the pain demands the recall of fond memories which tend to *diminish* psychic helplessness and suffering. In the process of mourning, the pleasures of the lost object's presence are psychically reexperienced alongside the pain of the loss and make the pain tolerable. The grief "fills the empty heart," so that the individual is not overwhelmed by the feelings of helplessness, loss, and rage.

In mourning, therefore, "working through" the loss results from the repetitious experience of the pain in association with the memories of the gratifications provided by the lost object. The reintegration of the object representation takes place in the *fantasied* presence of the lost object. Mourning causes the memory to stay awhile, so that the bereaved can say, "Goodbye."

If this line of reasoning is followed to a consideration of failures of the process of mourning, the dynamics of depression are brought into focus. Excessive ambivalence makes it impossible for the loss to be overcome. There are insufficient discharge-gratifications associated with relatively conflict-free memories, with the result that the grief cannot be worked through, just as the failure to establish and maintain the basic positive transference can cause the analytic process to fail. The pain persists, and the affective component of the depression continues to represent the attachment to the lost object. The paradoxical observation by some patients well along in analysis, that they experience a sense of "comfort" in the depressive affect, supports this conclusion.

During childhood, the ego is inadequate for dealing with serious separations, although substitute objects may minimize the effects of the experience of loss for varying periods of time. If the defensive forces of the ego are inadequate, then or later, there may be further dynamic regression to a narcissistic withdrawal, as Freud (1917) described in his description of "melancholia." In that sense, neurotic depression expresses a state in which the lost object is still ambivalently cathected, the depression expressing the attachment to the object and protecting against further regression of the ego. The discharge into consciousness of the affect associated with the lost object stimulates repeated, if unsuccessful, efforts to complete the process of mourning, while guarding against psychotic decompensation.

A different response may be observed when there is a fragile attachment to the object representation. Following a loss, there is an inability to grieve. If there is an organic predisposition, major psychosomatic reactions may occur (see Wallace, 1975).

The affects guilt and shame are closely related to depression. Beres (1966) noted that, "object loss leads to depression only when it is accompanied by ambivalence toward the lost object and subsequent guilt" (p. 497). There appears to be an even greater clinical affinity between shame and depression. This would be expected from the observation that shame is related genetically to earlier conflict and would tend to be less effective as a signal affect. Brenner (1975), in fact, classified shame as a depressive affect. Shame is differentiated from humiliation in that the latter reflects a failure in the defensive function of shame with the result that there is a fusion of shame and depression along with a sense of hopelessness.

Beres (1966) also emphasized the importance of differentiating other affective responses from depression, such as sadness, apathy, grief, and unhappiness. The latter affective states describe *current* frustrations and disappointments, regardless of the extent to which they are predetermined by unconscious factors. The persistent affective state described as "depression" is closer to unresolved mourning reactions.

Apathy can accompany a depressive affect or occur independently. When it is associated with depression—and it is often an important part of the clinical picture—it reflects a hopeless attachment to a lost object; however, the attachment persists. In the absence of the depressive affect, apathy may express the loss of the attachment to the object representation and may then become a symptom of psychotic withdrawal.

Boredom also frequently accompanies depression, and it often requires a parallel major focus in the treatment. Boredom is the affective response to (internal or external) inhibition of the pursuit or experience of satisfaction (Fenichel, 1945). The tension that is associated with ambivalence is more apparent than with apathy. Depression and boredom often participate in the clinical picture in a reciprocating interaction, each contributing to the intensification of the other.

To summarize, anxiety describes the affective response to the anticipation of a frustrating experience (Freud, 1926). Shame, guilt, and depression and its related affects can be conceptualized as parallel phenomena that accompany the incomplete integration of ego identifications. Shame accompanies the ambivalent identifications associated with preoedipal attachments. Its primary anxiety is the fear of loss of a love object, but it carries complex fantasies associated with its genetic roots.

Guilt, likewise, derives from ambivalent identifications associated with later attachments, especially those of the oedipal stage. The parallel anxieties reflect the phallic stage of development, including castration fear and loss of love.

Depression is associated with both shame and guilt, and it requires as a precursor only the establishment of some degree of attachment, that is, some basic ego development. All three reflect adaptive responses of the ego to frustration. They provide psychic discharge phenomena associated with ambivalent imagos that function to stabilize the ego. In this context, the libidinal aspect of the ambivalence is crucial to the homeostatic functions that help sustain psychic structure.

Part II

THE THERAPEUTIC PROCESS

INTRODUCTION

The following three essays offer a further discussion of the therapeutic process within the perspectives of the preceding theoretical formulations. These are edited versions of previously published papers that have been adapted for this volume.

It seems to me that the clinical concepts emerged first in my thinking. As I became increasingly aware of the function of gratification during the course of my work with my patients, the development of the theoretical views helped me to organize my ideas about the therapeutic process. In any case, the two series of essays belong together. The theoretical and clinical aspects of psychoanalysis should provide a coherent, integrated picture. I have attempted to achieve this within the framework of the basic metapsychological and clinical viewpoints.

The first of the clinical papers, "The Psychoanalytic Situation and the Transference Neurosis," was published in *The Israel Annals of Psychiatry and Related Disciplines* (Volume 12, pp. 304–318) in 1974. The evolution of the patient's responses to the gratifications of the analytic situation is described here and provides the bases for schematically dividing the course of psychoanalysis into four overlapping stages: (1) initial rapport; (2) turbulence related to conflicts associated with the basic transference; (3) stable transference neurosis with working through of neurotic conflicts; and (4) termination and separation.

The second clinical paper, "The Transference Neurosis and the Therapeutic Process," was published in the *Journal of the Philadelphia Association for Psychoanalysis* (Volume 6, pp. 39–52) in 1979. Some aspects of the relationship between technique and the development of therapeutic insight are considered, especially in the context of the gratifications to the patient in the therapeutic interaction. The development of increasing levels of insight is examined in order to better understand its role in the therapeutic process.

The third essay, "Silence, Sleep and the Psychoanalytic Situation," was also published in the *Journal of the Philadelphia Association for Psychoanalysis* (Volume 7, pp. 61–88), in 1980. It offers a more detailed examination of gratification and frustration of the patient in psychoanalysis, along with a further integration of technique and the therapeutic process, with emphasis on the significance of the "oral triad" described by Lewin in 1950. The most primitive bases of the analytic interaction are described, both in terms of their productive aspects as well as countertransference problems they may mobilize. I examine Kohut's self psychology in the context of these views and conclude that the narcissistic clinical phenomena he described can be understood better—and treated more effectively—within the framework of Freud's conflict theory of neurosis.

4

THE PSYCHOANALYTIC SITUATION AND THE TRANSFERENCE NEUROSIS

Psychoanalysis is experienced by the patient as a series of psychological events leading to insight and modifications of the patient's habitual neurotic responses. In order to achieve this, the analyst provides an environment which is conducive to the development of a transference neurosis and its resolution by interpretations alone (Gill, 1954). This "environment," the psychoanalytic situation, provides sublimated gratifications which help make it possible for the patient to tolerate the frustrations of the transference neurosis and to master the underlying conflicts by means of the analytic experience.

The major contribution of the analyst to the psychoanalytic situation is provided by his neutral stance which establishes the basis for a reciprocal relationship with the patient. The neutrality reflects a noncritical attitude to the patient's associations, but it does not imply an attitude of neutrality to the patient. On the contrary, the analytic stance of neutrality resembles closely, in its psychological implications, the abiding attention and constancy of care of the parents of an infant. The participation by the analyst requires an intense, if limited, emotional attachment to the patient in order to sustain the quality of attention and the capacity for a reciprocal response with the patient's evolving ego. It is the analyst's capacity to offer his patients this kind of sublimated love that determines his suitability for

analytic work, and which permits him to provide the impetus that is necessary to reestablish an external influence
on the patient's evolving ego.

These considerations regarding the analyst's involve-
ment with his therapeutic task, and the significance of the
patient's reciprocal responses, were implied by Freud
(1913):

> When are we to begin making our communications
> to the patient? . . . Not until an effective transference
> has been established in the patient, a proper *rapport* with
> him. It remains the first aim of the treatment to attach
> him to it and to the person of the doctor. To ensure this,
> nothing need be done but to give him time. If one ex-
> hibits a serious interest in him, carefully clears away the
> resistances that crop up at the beginning and avoids
> making certain mistakes, he will of himself form such an
> attachment and link the doctor up with one of the imagos
> of the people by whom he was accustomed to be treated
> with affection. [p. 139–140]

The genetic determinants for these experiences of gratification are believed to derive from the comfort of the
early mother-child relationship. The influence of these
primordial gratifications on the evolution of the transference neurosis and their effects on the therapeutic process
is the subject of this investigation. The patient must achieve
the capacity to accept such gratifications in order to attain
the clinical transference neurosis, and they are necessary
for the patient to tolerate and eventually master the anxieties associated with his warded-off impulses and fantasies
during the process of working through.

Greenacre (1968) focused on these gratifications in her
discussions of the basic transference:

> My own clinical observations led me to consider that

this basic transference relationship had its roots in the earliest mother-infant bond and reproduced the helpless infant's primitive trust in the need-fulfilling mother. . . . On first consideration, this basic element in the transference appeared to me as a regressive revival of infantile dependence. Subsequent reflection brought the further idea that the mere existence of such a need for relationship is not, in itself, necessarily regressive, since it is an essential ingredient for the maintenance of life itself in infancy and is a necessary component in all later productive activities in life. It certainly contains strong regressive pulls in the situations of suffering, which together with the limitations of the analytic situation, act to extrude the transference neurosis. It may also catalyze the therapeutic alliance at the same time that its regressive elements act as contaminants. Perhaps one may say that it is the continuous viability of this first slight step of conversion of primary narcissism into the very beginning of object relationships which must be retained if object relationships are to develop and withstand untoward conditions later in life. [p. 212]

To this she added, "The analyst thus supplements the patient's self-observing and self-criticizing functions and may operate almost as though he were a part of the patient" (p. 214).

This primordial response in the patient's basic transference is the obverse of the analyst's neutral stance. If we agree with Greenacre's comment that this "need for relationship . . . is a necessary component in all later productive activities in life," the analyst is observed to use his own need for relationship within the confines of the analytic situation to stimulate that same need in the patient. Regardless of the restrictions imposed by the treatment, the analyst must offer himself as a person to whom the patient can respond, and his earliest interpretations must relieve the early resistances to this primordial response in the basic transference.

The rule of abstinence, in turn, refers to the necessity for the analyst to avoid submitting to the patient's demands for satisfaction of instinctual drive derivatives associated with neurotic conflict. It does not suggest the creation of an artificial atmosphere of coldness or "abstinence" in the psychoanalytic situation. The gratifications to the patient are necessary for the development of the transference neurosis, even as the frustrations determine the quality and content of the neurosis in the transference neurosis. (The rule of abstinence is discussed at greater length in chapter 6.)

The evolution of the primordial gratifications in the basic transference can be used *schematically* to divide the course of psychoanalysis into four overlapping stages: (1) that of initial rapport; (2) a turbulent stage of transference neurosis with a working through of the conflicts associated with the primordial gratifications; (3) a stable transference neurosis characterized by a relatively conflict-free primordial attachment to the analyst during which there can be some effective working through of neurotic conflicts; and (4) termination and separation. A clinical report will be used to demonstrate this schematic reconstruction.

Case Report

The patient was a twenty-two-year-old, recently married woman who presented herself with a request for psychoanalysis, based on a feeling that there was "something wrong" with her, although she couldn't define it. There was a lack of satisfaction in everything she did, she was unable to find any direction, and she felt that she didn't know "who" she was.

A history of disturbed behavior leading to prostitution

and cocaine habituation appears to have been the expression of a severe adolescent identity crisis that was complicated by drug abuse. However, she had spontaneously discontinued drugs and rehabilitated herself before she consulted me, suggesting that she was ready to go beyond this 'temporary upheaval in her life, even though she needed some help.

The patient had left home shortly after finishing high school, where she had become a heavy user of marijuana. She eventually moved to Hollywood, with the conscious desire "to experience everything." She tried many drugs, but avoided heroin and LSD. For a period of two or three years, she took intravenous cocaine frequently, and she may have been addicted. She affiliated with a black procurer who had one other girl working for him, a black lesbian. The patient left him several times, but returned after short periods.

She also became involved in a check-forging ring and was eventually apprehended and convicted of a felony. It was evident that she had caused herself to be caught by returning to the site of a previous forgery with another forged check, just one day later. When taken into custody she deliberately closed the book on her past by giving detailed information to the police about the check-forging ring. She knew, then, that she would be killed if she returned, and for a time she lived in realistic fear that her erstwhile confederates might locate and kill her.

While involved in prostitution, she had arranged to be a paid mistress for a middle-aged businessman. He offered to marry her, and while she was making up her mind he sent her to a finishing school in Switzerland for a year. On her return, she resumed contacts with her procurer as well as her use of drugs, until her arrest for forgery. Since this was her first offense, she was released on probation. Feeling desperate and in need of help, she married the older man, knowing that he was but a temporary port in a storm.

During the initial interview the patient described herself as a happy, easygoing person; but when she talked about herself she burst out crying, which she could not understand. The crying was actually appropriate to the events she was describing, but she hadn't realized they had affected her so much. It soon became clear that this was a manifestation of the major symptom that brought her into treatment, her depression.

The second interview was four days later, and she reported that she had her husband's permission to begin analysis and wanted to start. She added further history of her need to please and to be loved. She enjoyed the challenges of acquiring love from others; but periodically she felt "overwhelmed" and withdrew into total isolation for a few days. She knew that this desire to be liked would make it difficult to talk freely to me, but she wanted to proceed.

The patient seemed desperate for help, she demonstrated a fair degree of psychological-mindedness, and I felt some rapport developing. So we began psychoanalysis, five visits per week. This frequency continued for about three years, when we decreased to four visits per week for the last two and a half months.

During the first analytic hour, the patient reported a dream: There were two military men in uniform. She was on an island, and there was a room to eat in. They had to say a code word to get on a launch for a trip to the mainland. She heard one of the men say the code word to the other, a French word like "excellent," and this surprised her. People were smiling. The boat was "easily accessible."

The patient associated that the island was the way she "visualized time." In retrospect, this represented the segment of time involved in her identity crisis, and the analysis represented the return to normal life. One of the military men wore a cap like the one her father wore when she was a child. She was his favorite of the three children and used to go fishing in a boat with him until she reached her teens. This was clearly a transference dream and expressed the patient's readiness to transfer positive feelings from her father onto me. At the time, it was a hopeful sign, indicating an evolution of positive rapport. Later, it became the basis of a transference resistance, when she defended against erotic fantasies by putting me "on a shelf, alongside of Father," as the only two men who were not prey to her seductive efforts.

By the end of the first week of analysis, the patient had reported enough childhood history to completely and finally destroy her fantasy of a "happy childhood." Her rivalry with, and hatred of, her younger brother was so intense that she had consciously planned to kill him when they grew up, and she terrified him by telling him so. Her mother was occupied with her own mother's gradual deterioration from multiple sclerosis over many years, causing her to neglect her children. There were a number of deaths of close relatives during childhood, and the patient developed major defenses of denial in order to ward off her fear of dying. When I summarized the evidence against the "happy childhood," the patient developed a headache and cried.

Dreams were soon reported which described sexual relations with older men, with ambivalent feelings that were poorly disguised. However, the deeper conflicts with her mother as the principal object in her neurosis also began to appear. It soon became evident that the patient's mother had encouraged the patient to be the "free spirit" that the patient imagined herself to be. She knew from early childhood that she was expected by her mother to throw off the bonds of conventionality that had inhibited

her mother and to "experience everything." The identification with her mother's unconscious but obvious fantasies became an important insight early in the analysis.

During the first few weeks the specific conflicts manifested a fluid quality during the analytic hours. I repeatedly interpreted her struggle to ward off affects and the
association of this with her boredom, which she described
as a major chronic symptom. I also interpreted the relation
of her idealized impulsive behavior to the inevitable frustration and her lack of a sense of identity. She described
the quality of her object relations as based on an effort to
be what someone wanted: "More than half of me is trying
to find out what the next person wants me to be, and be
that . . . constantly assuming a new role." This gave her
"control" over others, including her former "tricks" when
she was a prostitute, without allowing a "need" to develop
for the other person. She said that she felt lost with me,
because I didn't provide her with clues about what I wanted
her to be.

Transference conflicts gradually appeared. When her
associations led in that direction, I demonstrated to her
that her habit of repeatedly coming late was a compromise
between her growing interest in the analysis and her re-
sentment at the invasion of privacy and loss of independ-
ence that this involved. She stated that she was angry when
I was right; but for a period of time she stopped coming
late and missing hours. Subsequently, she described a feeling of "seething" inside, associated with "ironic laughter"
and the feeling that she was mocking me. There were
dreams of seeing men nude from behind, and toilets ov-
erflowing with feces. During this time she became more
aware of the anger and hatred that she carried within her.

One day, after she had missed the previous hour with
a poor rationalization, she reported that she had "missed"
me and her hour, and she was angry at me because she

didn't like to feel dependent. There was a spontaneous lifting of repression with affect, and she recalled childhood memories of being forbidden to go into her parents' bedroom.

She then began to struggle against the fantasied danger of sexual feelings toward me. She began to consider acting out in an extramarital affair, which she could understand intellectually as an effort to ward off sexual feelings toward me.

One Friday she reported intense, depressing boredom. She had dreamed there was a hungry stray dog in front of a movie. She picked it up and rushed home to feed it, and it ate an enormous amount. She was happy watching it eat and knew it was going to get better.

She associated "rushing" to her rush to complete the analysis as my best patient, before I discovered how empty she was and that she had nothing to offer. She wanted to feed me her success so that I would not be hurt and disappointed in her. Then she associated her own hunger for love, and she felt like a child, small, and that I was "far away, at the other side of the room," although she knew that I was sitting close to her. When I asked her associations to the movie, she responded that it was the movie she attended on Friday nights as a teenager. I interpreted that she would feel lonely not seeing me over the weekend, and that this was associated with the feelings of boredom and depression. She agreed and went on to associate about her fear of sexual feelings toward me that would frustrate her. I sensed her fear of the opposite, that she would seduce me sexually and then lose me. At first she denied it, but then concurred and spoke of how she had seduced so many men, so easily, and afterward had "felt used," even though she had initiated it. I added that this was what she feared with me. Her response was that this was correct, and that since I had put this into words she felt relieved, and with this the boredom passed.

During the next week she described a feeling of keeping things from me, but she didn't know what. No insights emerged; but at the end of the week she reported with surprise that she felt that her "princess" fantasy of doing everything she pleased on impulse no longer appealed to her; she had become interested in carrying out various responsibilities that she had undertaken. She added that the desires for impulsive action were still there, but they were alien to her, now, for the first time. This frightened her. What if she gave up that image of herself and there was nothing to replace it?

The behavioral difficulties and problems of acting out were far from resolved at this time. Yet the development of this ego-alien quality was a significant turning point early in the analysis and marked the transition from neurotic transferences in the analysis to the beginning of the transference neurosis. From then on her impulsive action was clearly a reaction to developing transference fantasies which could be analyzed in the context of the transference neurosis.

Shortly after this, there was an hour in which the patient abreacted the grief and horror of her mother's catastrophic illness. Almost five years had elapsed since her mother's diagnosis of cancer. There had been recurrences, and it was known she was dying, although still functioning in her own home. Irradiation therapy and anticancer drugs were keeping her alive.

When the patient returned to this subject, I interpreted her defense against her feelings about her mother's illness. The patient became racked with grief, sobbing bitterly while asserting, "I can't stand it. I can't stand it. It's not fair." Her weak efforts to reestablish her defenses of denial were easily penetrated now, and the patient faced for the first time her overwhelming sense of horror at her mother's illness and her own inability to tolerate the prospect of her mother's death. Following this, the patient began to establish a new relationship with her mother, became her mother's friend and confidante, and was very supportive to both parents during the terminal illness later in the analysis. The patient's grief at the time was normal and appropriate, and led to the recognition that she missed her mother and carried much of her mother with her.

After the hour of the hungry-puppy dream, which I felt marked the beginning of the transference neurosis, the patient repeatedly experienced a sleepy relaxation on the couch. The analysis of this state was most helpful in understanding the dynamics of the basic transference. Although she never fell asleep, there was a kind of regression which symbolized sleep to the patient. She felt like going to sleep. It represented the displacement of her drug addiction onto the analytic situation, and suggested the beginning of an addictive object relationship which repeated the conflicts that she had experienced with her former procurer. She had repeatedly returned to him after separations, completely submissive and, she reported, with a feeling of being a projection and manifestation of his being. She would collapse "like a wet rag," to be used in whatever way he saw fit. After a period of time she would rebel and leave him again for an independent existence.

The analytic situation stimulated the same response, the feeling of total submission in her sleepy state, followed by the inevitable anxiety which she relieved by acting out. The desire for cocaine had represented an expression of the same wish for fusion with an idealized object but under her own control. She recognized that this included the wish for death. Moreover, her desire for sexual intercourse included the same fantasy, of fusion with an idealized object.

Later in the analysis, the patient was able to elaborate

on the meaning of the symbolic sleep on the couch. It represented a desire to "become one" with the couch, the analysis, and me. Only then, she felt, could she "take in" what I said.

When the patient began the analysis, she reacted as if she had to respond to every impulse. In retrospect, she realized that it had been inconceivable to her that she might have an urge and not act on it. Also, as far as her conscience was concerned, the impulse and the action were the same. In another sense, an idea that came from someone else was treated the same as if it were her own impulse, and she had to act on it if it appealed to her.

The struggle to control her impulses paralleled in the analysis the working through of her conflicts about dependent feelings and merger fantasies in regard to me. As the struggle reached a peak, there was a crisis in the analysis. When I took some time off after Christmas, the patient moved in with a boyfriend and stayed away from the analysis for a week after my return. This jeopardized her marriage and her husband's cooperation in the analysis. She later reported that it was at this time that she "decided" to stop fighting her dependence on me; and the major acting out with boyfriends stopped abruptly. Prior to this, she felt that I was somebody she disliked, and the analysis was like "taking bad medicine."

Now I became somebody that she "liked." A word became important to her—"alternatives." Previously she had none, since she was driven to act on every impulse. Now there was a discovery that there were alternatives, to act or not to act, and to think.

The patient became fully committed to the analysis. She lived only for the one interest, to spend her hour each day with me. Since her husband's job involved public relations and frequent social contacts, she became adept at handling these chores and felt that she earned his support for the analysis.

She became aware of problems regarding her feminine self-image and worked through some aspects of her sexual confusion and masculine identification. This was associated with the disturbed relationship between her parents, her identification with aggressive elements in her mother's personality, and identifications with her father, as well as penis envy involving her brother and father.

The patient also became aware of the narcissistic qualities of her romantic fantasies. She stated, "My last lover was a great big statement of my egoism. It was loving myself, an obsession." She could recognize the "lofty feeling" of romantic love and see the danger in it. She felt now that she did not have to "rush into bed" in pursuit of her romantic fantasies.

The need to be alert to the needs of others in order to be what they wanted apparently became transformed into an increasing capacity for empathy.

At this time, the patient began to see me more as a "real person" that she was fond of. Transference distortions diminished, and she met a suitable person for possible marriage and became emotionally involved with him. To her surprise, there was a different kind of orgasm with him. She described it as much deeper, spreading to take over her entire body. Formerly, orgasm had been experienced only near the outside of her genital area. She said that she had read about "vaginal orgasm" as being different from clitoral (I hadn't spoken of this), but she hadn't believed it. Now she realized that she had formerly felt that the erect penis was like a hook stuck into her. She had previously expressed her preference for fellatio and cunnilingus; now she understood better why this was so.

The patient's concept of sexual fidelity had also changed. Before, the idea had meant a restriction on her behavior.

Now it was felt to be a choice that *she* made. She had planned to develop her talents as a writer, and she felt that she would have become a strong advocate of "Women's Lib." Now she felt that this was a foolish struggle. At the termination of analysis she had developed a strong desire to marry and raise children.

Discussion

A single case report obviously cannot provide convincing evidence in itself of common denominators in psychoanalytic treatment. This case was selected because of its suitability for illustrating my thesis.

The history suggested that the initial rapport was an expression of an emotional investment in the analyst that stimulated the beginning of the therapeutic process. The transference neurosis with its acting out became established when there was an addiction to the analyst that expressed the fantasy of the reestablishment of psychic union with an omnipotent parent. The transference neurosis became stabilized when the fantasies associated with the addiction became relatively conflict-free, and led to the final stages of treatment in which the addictive transference was relieved. It must be acknowledged, however, that most cases do not develop in such an orderly manner, and there is always considerable overlapping of the stages. Also, the turbulent stage of the transference neurosis need not be experienced to the same extent by all patients, some of whom may have sufficient capacity for the necessary attachment in the basic transference so that a stable transference neurosis evolves gradually out of the initial rapport.

Each stage of the transference has significant therapeutic implications. Rapport may often be recognized from the first hour and, I believe, expresses the beginning of a mutual attachment between patient and analyst. From the analyst's side, it is felt as sensitivity to the dynamic processes of the patient and an ability to communicate them. He feels able to carry out the tasks associated with the "neutral stance" of the analyst.

The quality of rapport is stimulated in the patient by appropriate confrontations of preconscious processes, not on the basis of theoretical formulations, but as statements by the analyst that reveal to the patient his recognition of the patient's inner life. The patient responds with a sense of trust and, within the limitations of his neurosis, a readiness to work with the analyst. It is this response that offers evidence of the patient's healthy ego that is initially available for the analysis and provides a major indicator of prognosis for analytic treatment. In this we are discussing the core of the healthy ego that provides the foundation for a therapeutic relationship.

The initial rapport was expressed in the first dream. The good feelings at the beginning of the boat trip in the dream were directly associated with pleasant experiences with her father. It initiated the "honeymoon stage" of analysis where so much therapeutic work often appears to be accomplished, until transference conflicts appear and destroy the illusion of magical treatment.

Still, while under the influence of the early rapport the patient was able to reexamine her conscious memories of her childhood, to become aware of some of the anger she carried with her, to examine the qualities of her character, and to recognize the influence of her mother's fantasies on her own identity as a "free spirit." All of this provided a statement of the analytic task and led to the transference conflicts associated with dependency.

As a general rule the quality of analytic work based on rapport is limited to this kind of development. The responses in the basic transference are similar to those manifested by every person as soon as there is a significant emotional investment in an object relationship. Until the transference neurosis is achieved, the transference reactions fail to reach the intensity and quality that permits significant lifting of repression, the working through of basic conflicts, and the penetration of screen memories. When treatment is limited to this level of transference some patients can achieve significantly increased awareness of their inner lives with some working through of derivative conflicts. A new psychic homeostasis may be established that is relatively free of the symptoms that brought the patient into treatment (for an example of this result see Wallace, 1969). However, therapeutic insight involving significant ego modifications and character changes are generally not achieved unless a full transference neurosis is established and worked through.

According to Freud (1914a), the transference neurosis differs from casual transferences in that the neurosis becomes focused on the analyst to the relative exclusion of manifestations outside the analysis. As the first portion of the analysis preceding the transference neurosis reached its peak, my patient was faced with her conflicts regarding dependency and associated erotic and destructive fantasies. During the hour of the hungry-puppy dream, her affects became "frozen" into the quality of boredom that had caused her a great deal of distress in the past. Interpretations of preconscious seduction fantasies unfroze her affects sufficiently so that the dependent attachment could continue to evolve into the beginning of the transference neurosis. This was accompanied by the sleepy relaxation on the couch and by a great deal of acting out.

According to Rangell (1968b), acting out differs from other neurotic action in that it represents a "resistance, at any phase along the road of analysis, based upon anxiety occasioned by the efforts of the latter to achieve successful and *effective* insight by the undoing of previously repressed mental content" (p. 196).

Until such behavior expresses a displacement from the transference, it should not be termed "acting out" in the analytic sense. When it does, it represents a disturbance in the evolution of the transference neurosis. In my patient, it demonstrated that the behavior disorder, which had been somewhat controlled during the stage of rapport, had entered the analysis as an expression of the transference neurosis. It soon became evident that her turbulent behavior masked and defended against the primitive infantile conflicts associated with her addiction. The ambivalence associated with these specific conflicts, I believe, provoked the subsequent extreme acting out.

This turbulent stage of the transference describes the period during which conflicts surrounding the basic transference disturb the transference neurosis and predispose to acting out. It expresses the psychopathology of a drug addiction transferred onto an object relationship. The case report reveals the extent to which these conflicts jeopardized the therapeutic relationship and very nearly destroyed the analysis.

The positive therapeutic aspects of the ambivalence were reflected in the fact that my patient's behavior disorder developed an ego-alien quality. Previously, she had been in treatment because of the pain caused by her neurosis. Now, she was in analysis because of her attachment to the analyst and could begin to integrate the interpretations. It was not until later that the patient described how this was made possible by the merger fantasy that was symbolized by sleep on the couch.

It appears that the desire to sleep represented an expression of the infantile wish for reunion with the idealized mother that is observed in all of our patients, and it had to be reexperienced in order to make contact with the associated fantasies. Then she could begin to describe the transference wish for and fear of merging with the analyst and to connect this with her neurosis.

With some patients, especially those who are very disturbed or borderline, the major part of treatment may be devoted to working through a turbulent transference neurosis of this type. If this becomes excessively prolonged, it is sometimes necessary to settle for partial resolution of this basic conflict. It requires a substantial core of healthy ego in our patients to work through this stage of analysis.

In my patient, when the conflicts surrounding the merger fantasies were sufficiently worked through, the foundations for object relations were reestablished and a stable transference neurosis was achieved. Does it carry an analogy too far to consider the stable transference neurosis as a conflict-free addiction—that is, as an addiction in the service of the ego? When we consider the intense emotional investment by our patients in the analysis during this stage, the craving for dependent gratifications within the analytic setting, and the psychic discomfort when the satisfactions provided by the psychoanalytic situation are, for any reason, delayed, we observe a clinical situation which appears dynamically similar to an addiction. Furthermore, the psychopathology of the addiction that was uncovered by the analysis had identical genetic roots as those described by Greenacre for the basic transference. As soon as these derivatives of "the earliest mother-infant bond" became attached to the analyst, the patient was able to respond to the interpretations as if they came from within and to begin to work through the underlying conflicts.

As a result of the preceding analytic work, my patient was able to sustain an addictive attachment that is characteristic of all love relationships, in a stable transference neurosis. Then she reexperienced the infantile conflicts associated with her residual neurosis in the transference, as is characteristic of this stage. It appeared that the stable, addictive transference neurosis catalyzed the therapeutic process in two ways: first, by mobilizing the neurotic conflicts in the analytic setting; second, by providing gratifications which made the frustrations of the transference neurosis more tolerable, so that they could be worked through. Until the basic transference was stabilized in the transference neurosis, the remaining neurotic conflicts were not focused within the analytic situation in such a way that they could be worked through.

The change in the quality of the transference at this time suggested an identification with the neutral stance of the analyst that reflected the results of working through the previous turbulent transference neurosis. At this time there was a decrease in the manifestations of the neurosis outside the analysis, and the childhood origins of the neurosis were readily mobilized within the transference. The patient had increasing contact with her unconscious, with the result that she did more of the analyzing herself, not as a resistance, but as a consequence of diminishing resistance.

With patients for whom this development is possible, I believe that four or five visits per week are generally necessary. Then, when the sublimated satisfactions to the patient are stabilized in the transference neurosis, the therapeutic situation achieves its greatest therapeutic impact. Regardless of residual neurotic compromises, it stimulates the capacity for deep introspection and empathy and provides an extra dimension in object relations that is rarely present without deep analysis. This qualitative result is rarely, if ever, possible without the development of a stable transference neurosis.

In the usual course of events, when a full addictive transference is being worked through, the transference distortions gradually diminish and the sources of the attachment to the analyst become more available for object relations outside the analysis. In other words, the addiction to the analyst has come to be in the service of the ego rather than of the id, and it becomes available for object relations outside the treatment. The final separation produces sadness rather than symptoms. This does not imply that all unconscious conflicts have been worked through, but rather that those conflicts that were available for analysis at that time in the patient's life have been dealt with to a reasonable extent. In my patient, it remains to be seen whether the future anticipated stresses of life will mobilize latent conflicts requiring further analysis.

We can summarize by stating that the psychoanalytic situation establishes the conditions for the development of a psychic addiction which appears to be a precondition for the transference neurosis. The addiction recreates the conditions in which the patient's ego emerged from the infantile unstructured state, reestablishing useful contact with his inner life and enhancing his capacity for empathic object relations.

This may also hold the explanation for the fact that advocates of divergent schools of thought report significant therapeutic gains. If a relatively conflict-free addiction to the analyst develops, the gratifications to the conflict-free core of the ego often result in lasting therapeutic gains.

5

THE TRANSFERENCE NEUROSIS AND
THE THERAPEUTIC PROCESS

Psychoanalytic treatment involves two interacting and overlapping elements: the establishment and maintenance of therapeutic rapport between patient and analyst, and the investigation of the patient's unconscious conflicts, especially as they are manifested in the transference. While the emphasis on therapeutic goals has changed historically from overcoming repression and abreaction to the optimum broadening of the patient's ego, the essential ingredients of the therapeutic interaction have remained the same.

In the previous essay I described four fluctuating and overlapping stages of transference during psychoanalytic treatment. This essay will provide a greater focus on the relationship between psychoanalytic technique and the development of insight in the therapeutic process.

Lipton (1977) has described distortions of Freud's technique by various analytic writers, (e.g., Kris, 1951) who advocated a more impersonal therapeutic interaction than Freud espoused. The result was that the role of the working positive transference became confused and psychoanalytic treatment suffered. These alterations of Freud's views were incorporated into "classical" analysis by many analysts, even though they represented a viewpoint not formulated by Freud.

Lipton also suggested that all aspects of the working

positive transference represent aspects of the "personal relationship" with the analyst, and that while essential to the analytic process, they fall outside of what is properly considered psychoanalytic technique.

The issue is more than one of technique, however, or of what lies outside of technique. This "personal relationship" is an essential aspect of the analyst's therapeutic influence. To exclude it from "technique" creates the danger of removing an essential focus of interpretation that deals with the evolution of the basic transference into the transference neurosis.

It may be that Fenichel's monograph, *Problems of Psychoanalytic Technique* (1941), has influenced the repudiation of Freud's ideas on this subject by many analysts. At some points it appears that Fenichel is in agreement with the approach described by Freud and supported by Lipton. For example:

> Even though he influence the transference through interpretations and not by any other means, nevertheless the analyst's attitudes are continually taking part in the process. It will depend upon the situation whether he reveal more or less friendliness in his tone of voice, in the content of his remarks, or to what extent he alternate between a more friendly and less friendly attitude. [p. 87]

At another point, however, Fenichel wrote,

> there is one form of transference we preserve as long as possible because it represents a good aid for us in our work, and that is the paradoxically so called rational transference. It too must at some time become a resistance. At that point our task becomes the dissolution of the transference in its more limited sense. [p. 93]

The "rational transference" of Fenichel, the "working

positive transference" of Freud, and the "basic transference" of Greenacre seem to be designations for the same process. Where Freud described this in terms of the healthy portion of the patient's ego, Fenichel described it as an expression of resistance that must eventually be overcome like any other neurotic reaction in the transference. If this were so, any "personal" relationship, as described by Lipton, would contribute to the potential resistance of the "rational transference" and should be avoided. Fenichel did not specifically state that he was taking exception to Freud's clinical views, but I believe he may have contributed to the abandonment of an important aspect of Freud's ideas, with no clinical justification.

The therapeutic stance that I believe to be most consistent with psychoanalytic understanding relies primarily on the repetition compulsion as a clinical phenomenon that stimulates the transference neurosis. The analyst needs only to overcome the primary resistances to the establishment of the therapeutic attachment, as Freud suggested, and the neurosis will then be repeated in the transference. An inference to be drawn from this, and one I believe confirmed by clinical experience, is that the forward movements of the therapeutic process are stimulated by gratifications of the conflict-free aspects of the transference, rather than by the frustrations that mobilize the neurotic transferences, as suggested by Macalpine (1950) among others. (This is discussed at greater length in chapter 6.)

The importance of gratification to the patient in the therapeutic interaction has also been described from various perspectives: Benedek's description (1938) of "emotional shelter" for the patient; A. Reich's "sublimated infantile gratifications" (1950); Erikson's "basic trust" (1959); Stone's views as set forth in *The Psychoanalytic Sit-*

uation (1961); and Fleming's "primordial transference" (1972).

The healthy portion of the adult ego, and only the healthy portion, can permit the kind of influence by an emotionally invested object that leads to emotional growth. This is true whether we are observing a therapeutic situation or a normal developmental process. The healthy ego of the patient is nurtured and sustained by the analyst's emotional investment in him. The latter does not abandon his autonomy or relinquish his judgment, in spite of the intensity of his attachment. That would represent a regressive manifestation of resistance. The analyst's maturity, in turn, is demonstrated by his ability to be influenced in his choice of confrontations by the patient's associations, as well as his ability to learn from them. The healthy, judging portion of the patient's ego requires this input from the analyst in order to be mobilized for an effective therapeutic interaction.

In order to develop and sustain the contributions of this positive transference to the treatment, the analyst is faced with the same dynamic considerations that are present in other emotionally significant relationships. It is axiomatic that the different result in the analytic setting is a consequence of the interpretations, which modify the frustrations associated with the patient's infantile demands. Otherwise the neurotic repetitions would go on endlessly as they do outside of treatment. The analyst's interpretations diminish the frustration and anger which are ordinarily experienced and which generally contribute to the development of symptoms. The result is that the basic transference is protected and is better able to sustain the patient's participation in the therapeutic process, even as the range of ego operations is broadened.

A clinical example will illustrate this point. A patient well along in analysis noticed that the previous patient was late in leaving my office, and she fantasied that that patient was consistently getting more time from me than she did. She became so angry that it became difficult for her to express herself. Her rationalization for her anger was that she was getting less time from me than my other patients were and so was being cheated.

Basing my interpretation on current associative material, I said, in effect: You are angry with me as you were with your mother when she stopped treating you like a baby and paid more attention to your baby brother. The patient resumed her associations and was able to contribute more information regarding her competitive strivings as well as her ambivalence toward her brother. She responded to the interpretation as if she felt: Since I am not a baby and you are not my mother, I don't have to be so angry and *I can continue to love you* even though I feel angry and jealous of your other patients.

The result was that the attachment to the analyst was reinforced and the childhood frustration reexperienced in a new way. This appeared to have a moderating effect on the frustrated impulses of her childhood, as if the analyst provided a substitute for the presence of a loving mother in a situation of frustration. The result of the interpretation was that the infantile wish for exclusive possession of the analyst was subjected to the patient's capacity for reality testing and permitted increasing separation of past and present.

The patient's anger, which had interrupted the flow of associations, represented an intrusion on the basic transference that temporarily disturbed the therapeutic interaction. The interpretation was validated, not only by the content of her associations, but by the resumption of her flow of associations. The former could have been an intellectual response related to a reinforcement of ego defenses; the resumption of the flow of associations leading to new insights indicated the reestablishment of the basic transference and the working relationship. In other words, if a conflict is worked through with the analyst as a transference object it will be demonstrated by a progressive alteration of the transference. This makes the attachment to the analyst less subject to conflict but does not imply its dissolution.

Loewald's important paper, "On the Therapeutic Action of Psycho-Analysis" (1960), also emphasized the therapeutic interaction between patient and analyst: "These are experiences of interaction comparable in their structure and significance to the early understanding between mother and child" (p. 24). The insight gained becomes "an integrative experience" for the patient's ego, leading to "higher levels of organization." A necessary condition for this integrative experience, Loewald added, is that "the patient, through a sufficiently strong 'positive transference' to the analyst, becomes again available for integrative work with himself and his world, as against defensive warding-off of psychic and external reality manifested in the analytic situation in resistance" (p. 26).

My description of the therapeutic interaction overlaps considerably with Loewald's. If I understand him correctly, I feel that it is necessary to emphasize that the "positive transference" that carries the therapeutic process forward is the expression in the transference of that portion of the patient's ego that Loewald says "becomes again available for integrative work with himself and his world."

Loewald describes one aspect of the therapeutic interaction by saying that "the analyst makes himself available for the development of a new 'object-relationship' between the patient and the analyst. The patient tends to make this potentially new object-relationship into an old one" (p. 17). I would add that, from the patient's side, this potential for a new object relationship implies a preexisting capacity for therapeutic rapport. It is catalyzed to become the "positive transference" that carries the treatment forward via the therapeutic interaction.

Another clinical vignette, this time from the beginning of an analysis, should help to demonstrate how the development of the basic transference contributes to the evolution of the transference neurosis.

A young married woman requested treatment because of severe depression along with a chronic sense of hopelessness about achieving any happiness in her life. She hated her mother consciously, but felt guilty and was extremely submissive to her. Her relationship to her husband was also quite submissive, although she initially denied any hatred toward him.

The first observed transference response occurred very quickly. When I noted her name and address at the beginning of the first interview I discovered that she lived in a relatively distant community, and I offered to refer her to an analyst much closer to her home. She had gotten my name from the psychoanalytic society, and there was no reason to anticipate that she would have any unusual expectations of me. She became even more depressed than when she first arrived because, as she explained later, she felt that I did not want to treat her and was abandoning her. I discovered later that an important factor in the development of her neurosis was the fact that her father had abruptly abandoned the family when she was eleven years old, and she had never seen him again. Her readiness for transference reactions was immediately apparent, but whether she could develop an analyzable transference neurosis remained to be seen.

By the end of the first interview the patient had chosen to enter treatment with me. As we began the analysis her initial transference responses reflected her current relationship with her mother. In the same way that she superficially acknowledged but did not believe anything her mother told her, she asked me broad theoretical questions about what made her "that way," while maintaining a passive attitude without any emotional participation in the interviews. I confronted her repeatedly with how similar this behavior was to her relationship to her mother.

The patient soon began to comment spontaneously about her inability to express any feelings during our sessions. She said that it was as if she were asking me to tell her what to feel. The only affect that she was able to experience was anxiety while in the waiting room, which she described as "natural" before seeing a doctor.

One day she complained that her son's pediatrician was often not available when she needed him. She went on to describe other physicians who had behaved badly to their patients. I interpreted that she also expected me to behave badly and to disappoint her. She confirmed this, adding that she was afraid I would abandon her when I discovered how bad a person she was.

Soon after, near the end of an hour in which she had been describing her intense loneliness even when her husband was present, she appeared on the verge of crying, suppressed it, and then wondered why she could not allow herself to cry while she was with me. Her father came to mind spontaneously, and she described him as never having cared for her or having shown any interest in her. However, the memories she described of the time before he left contradicted this characterization, and I confronted her with the discrepancy. She burst out crying and for the first time was able to acknowledge how much she missed him. She recalled, now, that she had loved him very much, in contrast to her previous expressions of indifference.

After this hour she spoke of my office as a "refuge," and of me as someone with whom she felt "secure." The anxiety she felt in the reception room was no longer "natural"; it had developed an ego-alien quality and could be brought into the treatment. Although the conflicts associated with her separation anxiety were far from resolved, it could be said that after several weeks the analyst began to be "linked up" with the affectionately charged image of her father.

The patient began to complain that she did not feel feminine, and she became concerned about her rather unfeminine manner of dressing. Even as she presented the problems associated with her feminine self-image she began to enjoy wearing more colorful clothes and changed her hair to a more feminine style. She also reported that she was more interested in sex with her husband. These events were recognized as emotional growth, even as the related conflicts began to focus on the analyst. She soon began to describe her feelings of antagonism toward all men, myself included.

In this clinical vignette there is evidence of an emerging transference neurosis: a sublimated positive transference associated with her father, and the invasion of this attachment by hostile and erotic elements that repeated some of her childhood conflicts. The establishment of the basic transference had moved the patient forward into areas of conflict that had been warded off by her regressive defenses. It could then become the major focus in her transference responses. The earlier passive response which simulated her relationship with her mother was also a transference repetition, but it did not express a transference neurosis whereby the neurotic conflict could become isolated in the transference and be given a new transference meaning. Instead it represented a resistance to the establishment of a basic transference.

The conflicts associated with her sexual identity which were mobilized by these events may have defended against preoedipal conflicts that were hinted at by her initial responses. That is not pertinent to my thesis, however. My confrontations regarding the similarity of her responses to me and to her mother helped to separate my image from that of her mother sufficiently for a useful thera-- peutic relationship to develop. After the basic transference was established it was necessary to focus on the new material which had been mobilized in the transference without, however, overlooking the defensive aspects of the material that suggested some fragility in the basic transference. In other words, the conflicts associated with the evolving basic transference had to be approached through the layering of defenses provided by the patient's neurosis. There was at this time an adequate core of healthy ego involved in the basic transference for the analysis to proceed.

The developing rapport with the analyst initially mobilized memories of her relationship with her father. When these became conscious they contributed reciprocally to the development of a firmer basic transference. This in turn stimulated the resumption of the growth of her feminine self-image which had apparently been disturbed by her father's disappearance. The result was evidence that the associated conflicts could be brought into the treatment in the form of a transference neurosis so that they could be worked through in turn.

Every intrusion of neurotic conflict into the basic transference does not create a stable transference neurosis, but generally requires some therapeutic intervention. This reinforces the basic transference as it increasingly isolates the neurotic conflict in the transference. Evolving insight helps the patient prepare for the resolution of conflict when the transference neurosis is fully established.

I believe that this sequence provides the prototype for the therapeutic process at each step in the development of therapeutic insight. Just as the initial development of the firm basic transference in the second patient stimulated a resumption of emotional growth with its accompanying conflicts, each firming up of the basic transference that accompanies a timely interpretation potentially stimulates further progress of a similar nature. Transference distortions can be modified by interpretations, and insight contributing to resolution of conflict is possible, I believe, only when the transference distortions and related conflicts become associated with a stable basic transference. Interpretations of conflicts that have not intruded on the basic transference generally do not provide the psychodynamic milieu for therapeutic impact. The various therapeutic maneuvers of the analyst—interpretations, confrontations, etc.—therefore have two implicit goals: to stabilize the basic transference and to work through neurotic conflicts as they intrude on it.

Each time a component of the neurosis is worked through, the patient may experience a mourning process that is related to relinquishing the infantile object associated with the conflict. This is often manifested clinically by the patient's paradoxical sadness over leaving behind a "part of himself." The analyst's presence, to the extent that he is the object of a firm basic transference, helps the patient to tolerate the loss.

The infantile objects associated with the neurotic conflicts also reflect ambivalent identifications. That is, the parental functions involved in the childhood experiences have not been integrated successfully into the ego. These, I believe, are replaced by identifications provided by the analyst in the therapeutic interaction. This process, like that in early childhood, leads to flexibility in contemporary relationships, so that the identifications with the analyst need not freeze the patient in various regressive aspects of the transference. The complex interaction involved in the process of working through, therefore, requires that the patient relinquish an infantile object that is involved in an ambivalent identification derived from frustrating interactions with his parents. The analyst provides the emotional support necessary for the patient to relinquish this object, and in so doing provides the source for new identifications that prepare the patient to leave the analyst.

Loewald (1960) likewise described the important role of identification in the integrative experiences of the therapeutic process. His view, however, appears to have incorporated the more traditional idea that the identifications with the analyst that contribute to the therapeutic progress are limited to the analyst's role as observer:

> The patient and the analyst identify to an increasing degree, if the analysis proceeds, in their ego-activity of scientifically guided self-scrutiny. . . .
> Early identification as part of ego-development, built up through introjection of maternal aspects, includes introjection of the mother's image of the child. . . .
> In analysis, if it is to be a process leading to structural changes, interactions of a comparable nature have to take place. [pp. 19–20]

The investigative role of the analyst, in any case, represents a manifestation in the therapeutic setting of his capacity for mature object relations, including the capacity for conflict-free attachment, commitment, and empathy. These qualities are conveyed to the patient not only by the analyst's role in the therapeutic interaction but by his selection of interpretations and the context in which they are made. These, I believe, combine to provide what Loewald calls the "higher level of organization" offered by the analyst in the therapeutic interaction. The patient moves toward this higher level of organization by means of the operation of the basic transference. As a result of successful analysis, the synthesizing function of the patient's ego leads to an integration of these aspects of the analyst's personality, even as it helps the patient to prepare to leave the analyst.

The termination of analysis involves a normal mourning process for the patient. If the basic transference is stabilized so that it develops the quality of an addiction, and if it is enhanced by working through a succession of transference neuroses, the attachment will be very strong as termination approaches. If the analysis has enhanced the range of the patient's ego sufficiently, however, the therapeutic gains will not be jeopardized. The analyst, of course, must be prepared to differentiate between the recurrence of depressive symptoms requiring additional analytic work, and the appropriate sadness as the patient leaves his longtime companion in the therapeutic relationship. The therapeutic identifications that evolve in the course of working through the neurosis prepare the patient for the final separation and make it possible. The last separation requires that the patient be identified with the analyst's role of observer, so that the self-analysis can continue in the analyst's absence. Even then, just as the child feels sad when he leaves his parents for his new life as an adult, the analytic patient feels sad when he finally leaves the analyst.

The sequence of events in psychoanalytic treatment from this perspective can be summarized as follows: The first function of confrontation and interpretation is to help separate the analyst from frustrating images from the past sufficiently to permit a latent sublimated attachment to be mobilized in the transference. Superficial confrontations and interpretations, especially of conscious affects and neurotic defenses, express the empathic quality and understanding of the analyst. This contribution from the healthy core of the analyst's ego stimulates the patient's reciprocal emotional investment in the analyst. Secondly, interpretations protect the emerging basic transference from the effects of excessive frustration so that it can continue to participate in the therapeutic process. This includes interpretations directed at conflicts associated with the roots of the basic transference. When the basic transference becomes stabilized, the gratifications to this healthy core of the patient's ego create a quality of a conflict-free addiction. This, in turn, facilitates the emergence of repressed (or otherwise warded-off) impulses to a preconscious level in association with the basic transference, so that the neurotic conflicts gradually become relatively isolated in the transference. This creates the transference neurosis.

The success of the process of working through results from the fact that the conflicts mobilized in the transference neurosis are reexperienced in a new psychological atmosphere provided by the stable basic transference. Each new insight that results from working through a neurotic conflict must lead to some modification of infantile urges. The effect is that they not only become available to the conscious ego, but that they can be gratified through contemporary adult behavior. Otherwise there would be no lasting therapeutic effect and the neurosis would recur. This implies a definition of *therapeutic* insight that requires a synthetic process in the ego. It includes, but is not limited to, an awareness of one's inner life. Insight can be designated therapeutic, therefore, only if it implies an integration of the understanding into the ego so that it provides the foundation for satisfaction and further growth. Therapeutic insight is both the result of the therapeutic process and its final step; it completes the task of separating past and present. The final effect of insight is to pass the adult function of judgment and reality testing onto the patient's ego. This requires a series of stable identifications with the analyst that ultimately help the patient leave the analysis.

It should be clear that I do not advocate anything like Alexander's "corrective emotional experience" as a substitute for therapeutic insight that results from the development and resolution of the transference neurosis by means of interpretation. The immediacy of the emotional experience in the transference that makes it convincing to the patient does not require role playing by the analyst. This aspect of the treatment situation, the object relationship between the patient and the analyst, can only be distorted by such maneuvers, which must inevitably intrude upon the integrative aspects of the treatment so necessary for its successful conclusion.

The patient's sublimated libidinal investment in the analyst and the gratifications provided by the analytic situation are essential aspects of the therapeutic process in psychoanalysis. A given patient's ability to be analyzed by a given analyst depends on whether this emotional investment can take place. Its success depends to a substantial degree on the analyst's ability to mobilize it by means of his own disciplined sublimated libidinal investment in the patient. Only by focusing on this aspect of the therapeutic interaction is it possible to resolve the conflicts associated with its development most successfully, and to transform the emerging insights into therapeutic changes.

6

SILENCE, SLEEP, AND THE
PSYCHOANALYTIC SITUATION

The Myth of the Silent Analyst

The functions of transference gratification and frustration
in the therapeutic process are at the heart of controversies
in both psychoanalytic technique and theory. The analyst
provides numerous gratifications to the patient within the
scope of his therapeutic activity through the expression of
his interest, especially its empathic quality, as well as by
means of anxiety-diminishing confrontations and interpretations. Of necessity, however, he has at his disposal
only one technique that may be experienced as a frustration by the patient. That is the judicious use of silence.
Regardless of his theoretical orientation, the analyst must
be silent while he listens, collects data, and attempts to
recognize patterns among the associative connections,
while he permits his own empathic and intellectual responses to emerge. Also, in a longitudinal time-sense, the
analyst must permit the emerging affects and fantasies of
the patient to reach a level of intensity such that the confrontations and interpretations will carry conviction. Finally, as the analysis progresses, the patient must be given
the opportunity to relive the emerging conflicts and to
integrate the therapeutic experiences at his own rate. It is
in these contexts that the analyst's silence inevitably is mis-
construed by the patient as a repetition of frustrating experiences out of the past.

The functions of the analyst's silence, however, have been grossly distorted by raising silence to the level of a therapeutic instrument. Lipton (1977) described this trend in his criticism of non-Freudian technique in "classical" psychoanalysis:

> The complaint that psychoanalysis is becoming "dehumanized" (Arlow, 1971) may be connected with just this tendency to substitute an encompassing technical instrumentality for a person. It can happen that the systematic application of this aspect of modern technique obscures the patient's capacity for establishing an object relationship and a transference neurosis and makes it appear that the patient suffered from a narcissistic disorder. This possibility broaches an important question, . . . the extent to which the frequency of narcissistic disorders, so much emphasized currently, is iatrogenic. [p. 266]

Lipton provided an important reminder that excessive frustration of the need for object relations distorts the clinical picture while imposing an iatrogenic regression on the patient. The abuse of silence has reached the proportion that there is a widespread belief in the "myth of the silent analyst."

This myth is readily observed among many patients. They anticipate silence from the analyst and may even express surprise at his participation in the analytic dialogue. This is commonly associated with grandiose fantasies that are projected onto the analyst, and that ordinarily defend against anxiety associated with negative transference. The analyst's presence is expected to stimulate the patient magically to achieve major insights and therapeutic changes. The patient's ambivalence may be expressed at the same time by a view of the analyst as an impassive individual who works like a machine that occasionally is activated to produce stereotyped interpretations. Patients who sidestep confrontations, or who regularly treat analytic confrontations as intrusions into their ideational patterns or who reject the concept of a psychoanalytic dialogue, represent a few of the most obvious resistances that may be reinforced by the image of the silent analyst. These responses ordinarily represent expressions of characterological defenses. Other patients deny the analyst's participation in the analytic dialogue after he has helped them achieve some therapeutic insight, sometimes as a manifestation of an emerging negative transference but also, at times, as a component of a negative therapeutic reaction.

A subtle expression of such resistance is manifested by patients who are willing to work with irrational transferences while avoiding responses to the analyst as a real person. They impose a "make-believe" quality on the therapeutic process so that the transference neurosis does not develop sufficiently to be therapeutically effective. The resulting apparent therapeutic changes do not last substantially beyond the termination of treatment unless the conflicts underlying the transference inhibitions have been resolved. With many such patients, tactful interpretations of resistances are initially perceived as reprimands by the analyst to stop some childish behavior and to become "better" patients. The implications of such responses should not be difficult to understand as manifestations of resistances that inhibit the development of an analyzable transference neurosis. However, I have observed this kind of ego-syntonic response at the beginning of second analyses, following treatment by well-trained analysts. This is not always a reflection of the patient's rigidity, nor even necessarily of the former analyst's failure to comprehend the patient's psychopathology. Treatment of these patients demonstrates that some analysts misunderstand the roles of gratification and frustration in the therapeutic process, especially in reference to the role of silence. They appear to be confused between the role of frustration as a stimulus for emotional growth and the conditions that make such growth possible. As a result, they appear to be confused regarding the relationship between therapeutic technique and the therapeutic process.

In what follows I will attempt to clarify certain aspects of the relationship between therapeutic technique and the therapeutic process in the context of the roles of gratification and frustration of the patient by the analyst. This is associated with the following questions: "How much" is optimal frustration for the patient in the analytic setting and, conversely, what represents optimal gratification? When does gratification of infantile needs reinforce neurotic regression and associated symptoms and inhibit therapeutic growth? In what way does gratification to the patient lead instead to the reinforcement of defenses and greater tolerance of anxiety, and does this contribute to the kind of personality reorganization ("ego growth") that psychoanalysis attempts to achieve?

These questions are related to the common observation that the infantile regressed state that is mobilized in the therapeutic setting is followed by emotional growth. Does this regression, therefore, provide the foundation for the resumption of the patient's emotional growth, or is it, as I believe, an expression of the growth experience that reveals the roots of the neurosis? Are the patient's infantile needs substantially satisfied in this regressed state, at least in his fantasies, as the basis of resuming emotional growth; or are the infantile fantasies mobilized for the purpose of demonstrating that they cannot be satisfied in contemporary life in order to educate the patient as to the benefit of abandoning the infantile goals that have been made conscious?

These questions, in turn, raise the issue of the proper

therapeutic stance and the question of what it is in the analyst's therapeutic activity that achieves his goals. If gratification of the patient inhibits therapeutic progress, how must the analyst offer interpretations empathically arrived at, when this empathic quality, in itself, nurtures the personal (object) relationship with the analyst? Conversely, since this nurturing cannot totally be avoided—with its supportive role for the patient—how do we demonstrate the validity of the interpretations themselves in the context of the therapeutic gains?

I have previously discussed the two interacting elements in the psychoanalytic situation that contribute to the development of the transference neurosis—the basic transference and the superimposed neurotic conflicts.

In the next section I will discuss the role of frustration to the patient in the contexts of the analyst's silence and the rule of abstinence. This will be followed by a discussion of the functions of gratification to the patient that are provided by the analyst's therapeutic stance. Then I will discuss some aspects of technique that are related to these issues and then go on to discuss further the functions of the basic transference in the context of the oral triad. The therapeutic approach recommended by Kohut will then be examined according to these frames of reference. Kohut's views are useful, also, as a contrasting viewpoint, which should help to bring my views into perspective.

The Rule of Abstinence

In his early papers on technique, Freud presented seemingly contradictory views on issues related to the analyst's therapeutic stance. At one point he wrote:

> I cannot advise my colleagues too urgently to model themselves during psycho-analytic treatment on the sur-

geon, who puts aside all his feelings, even his human sympathy, and concentrates his mental forces on the single aim of performing the operation as skillfully as possible. . . . The justification for requiring this emotional coldness in the analyst is that it creates the most advantageous conditions for both parties: for the doctor a desirable protection for his own emotional life and for the patient the largest amount of help that we can give him today. [1912b, p. 115]

Yet in another paper he had this to say:

When are we to begin making our communications to the patient? . . . Not until an effective transference has been established in the patient, a proper *rapport* with him. It remains the first aim of the treatment to attach him to it and to the person of the doctor. To ensure this, nothing need be done but to give him time. If one exhibits a serious interest in him, carefully clears away the resistances that crop up at the beginning and avoids making certain mistakes, he will of himself form such an attachment and link the doctor up with one of the imagos of the people by whom he was accustomed to be treated with affection. [1913, pp. 139–140]

Is it possible for a patient to develop an attachment to the doctor in which the latter represents an affectionate parent and provides the foundation for emotional growth when the doctor offers an attitude of "emotional coldness"? If Freud's first statement is considered as a one-sided approach to countertransference problems manifested by excessive sympathy from the analyst, it may have merit. As a principle of analytic technique, however, it can distort the patient's transference responses with the result that his collaborative efforts are based on primitive idealization rather than therapeutic rapport.

The two contradictory viewpoints are manifested in two

antithetical interpretations of the "rule of abstinence." Freud (1915a) described this rule as follows:

> The treatment must be carried out in abstinence. By this I do not mean physical abstinence alone, nor yet the deprivation of everything that the patient desires, for perhaps no sick person could tolerate this. Instead, I shall state it as a fundamental principle that the patient's need and longing should be allowed to persist in her, in order that they may serve as forces impelling her to do work and make changes, and that we must beware of appeasing those forces by means of surrogates. And what we could offer would never be anything else than a surrogate, for the patient's condition is such that, until her repressions are removed, she is incapable of getting real satisfaction. [p. 165]

One approach to psychoanalytic technique has evolved based on the conclusion that the transference neurosis develops as a result of the frustrations created by the rule of abstinence. Macalpine's paper on transference (1950) appears to have been a very influential statement of this point of view. "The transference neurosis," she wrote,

> may be defined as the stage in analysis when the analysand has so far adapted to the infantile analytic setting—the main features of which are the *denial of object relations* and continued libidinal frustration—that his regressive trend is well established, and the various developmental levels reached, relived, and worked through. [p. 529; italics mine]

The implication appears to be that regression to a stage of childhood or infantile conflict as a result of deprivation would stimulate the resumption of emotional growth, even though the analytic situation might repeat significant aspects of the original trauma. It is more likely that this would interfere with the patient's ability to recognize the regressive experience as a memory or to be helped to differentiate past from present.

The serious limitations of her presentation were, I believe, rationalized by the statement, "Only part of this way back from infantile levels to maturity falls within the time limit of analysis . . . ; the rest and the full adaptation to adulthood are most often completed by the analysand after termination of analysis" (p. 529). Macalpine's thesis implied that neither the concept of working through nor the principle of validation of interpretations by observations of emotional growth was essential to the formal analytic experience. Instead, she offered a somewhat hedged promise: "In this last postanalytic stage great improvements often occur" (p. 529).

Of those authors who have agreed with her point of view, I have selected two—Gill and Menninger—for comment. Gill's views are especially interesting because he subsequently reversed his opinion. In 1954, he agreed with Macalpine and went on to say, "Macalpine's account is especially illuminating because it stresses that the usual formula that the analytic transference is a spontaneous development is incorrect. The analytic situation is specifically designed to enforce a regressive transference neurosis" (p. 778). At that time, Gill emphasized that the frustrations of the analytic situation, including the silence of the analyst, were essential for the development of the "regressive transference neurosis." This, he said, was "related to the ambitious goal of psychoanalysis, to the need to actualize latent conflict . . . so that, if we do not enforce a regression, we shall not be able to come to grips with the deeper problems" (p. 779).

More recently, Gill (1979) presented an entirely different perspective.

If the analyst remains under the illusion that the current cues he provides to the patient can be reduced to the vanishing point, he may be led into a silent withdrawal, which is not too distant from the caricature of an analyst as someone who does indeed refuse to have any personal relationship with the patient. What happens then is that silence has become a technique rather than merely an indication that the analyst is listening. The patient's responses under such conditions can be mistaken for uncontaminated transference when they are in fact transference adaptations to the actuality of the silence. [p. 277]

I agree fully with this later statement. I think that it is likely that Gill as well as many other analysts intuitively rejected Macalpine's formulation in their clinical work, even while subscribing to it in theory. In 1961, Stone had already warned against the consequences of excessive detachment and withholding by analysts, although I think that the full implications of his monograph have been slow to evolve.

The "usual formula" regarding the spontaneous development of the analytic transference, which Gill had once been willing to replace, derives from the conflict theory of neurosis itself. When it is recommended that the induced frustrations of the analytic situation will "actualize latent conflict," a technique of treatment is proposed that bypasses interpretation of defense-resistance in favor of manipulation of the therapeutic environment. Freud (1916–1917) was quite explicit about this issue: "This work of overcoming resistances," he wrote, "is the essential function of analytic treatment; the patient has to accomplish it and the doctor makes this possible for him with the help of suggestion operating in an *educative* sense" (p. 451).

Certainly it is not a sufficient defense of a therapeutic approach to assert that Freud proposed it. However, if regression is mobilized by the methods of enforced abstinence as prescribed by Macalpine, the ego defenses are not brought into the sphere of transference interpretations, and the patient must be left without adequate understanding and insight into the defensive aspects of his mental operations, even if he discovers many genetic roots of the neurosis in his regressed state.

Menninger (1958) also described the therapeutic process in psychoanalysis as one in which regression is induced by the psychoanalytic situation in order to reach the point from which the patient resumes his growth. Menninger emphasized the silence of the analyst as a contributing factor in stimulating the regression. Yet, he acknowledged, "actually, of course, the patient is not denied anything except that which he should not have. . . . But the sense of frustration *experienced* by the patient is directly attributed by him (even against his better judgement) to what the analyst does and does not do—or say" (p. 53).

The subtlety of this problem is further indicated by Menninger's remark that "therapy is defeated by too rapid or too slow a regression or by too deep a regression too early in the treatment. . . . The analyst must learn to withhold, but he must also learn to give and to give at the right time" (pp. 53–54). Menninger correctly noted that frustrating the patient is not the therapy; yet he emphasized that the frustrating silence of the analyst in the early stages of treatment is an important element of technique for inducing a regression that must evolve into the transference neurosis.

If it were necessary to impose deprivations on patients in order to mobilize regressions that carry the infantile roots of their neuroses, why would they need to come for treatment in the first place? The regressive conflicts are already active in the patients' symptoms. The infantile needs, along with their repetitive disappointments, are expressed, however unconsciously, in every aspect of their

existence. The initial therapeutic task is to attach the neurotic conflict to the analyst where it can be manifested as
the transference neurosis. Then, interpretations of defense-resistance are most likely to mobilize the childhood
roots of the neurosis.

The therapeutic stance that is most consistent with
Freud's description of the rule of abstinence relies primarily on the repetition compulsion as a clinical phenomenon that stimulates the transference neurosis. The clinical
manifestation of the repetition compulsion is one of
Freud's most important and fundamental clinical discoveries, one not fully appreciated by many who advocate
revisions of his clinical approach. The neurotic patient
pursues the gratifications of frustrated childhood needs
in contemporary objects, but he repeats the failures of his
childhood in various disguises. The analyst needs only to
overcome the primary resistances to the establishment of
the therapeutic attachment, and the neurosis will then
inevitably be repeated in the transference neurosis, just as
it is repeated outside the treatment situation. In this view,
the development of the transference neurosis is not stimulated by the frustrations of the analytic setting, but by the
sublimated gratifications that lead to the primary attachment.

Adult derivatives of the instinctual drives that are expressed by the neurosis cannot be satisfied because of unconscious conflict, or else the patient would not come for
treatment. The rule of abstinence, therefore, derives from
the recognition that any effort to satisfy an *infantile* wish
must fail. The effort will, sooner or later, intensify the
frustration along with the neurotic defenses. Accordingly,
the application of the rule of abstinence has the paradoxical effect of helping to maintain the patient's frustrations
at a lower, more workable level. Its primary thrust is, simply, advice to the analyst not to distort the transference

neurosis by efforts to satisfy the patient's infantile wishes, including those disguised as adult wishes inappropriate to the analytic setting.

Transference Gratification

Neither theoretical stance necessarily overlooks the importance of the collaboration between the healthy portion of the patient's ego and the analyst. An emphasis on regression in the development of the transference neurosis, however, disregards the importance of the stable therapeutic attachment that Freud described as essential to the analytic process.

It is not enough to suggest that the patient's "healthy ego" is necessary for therapeutic success. The functions of the healthy ego are already impaired by the neurosis and do not operate most effectively in situations of induced deprivation. The analyst, I believe, must permit the healthy ego to be expressed in, and reinforced by, the attachment to the analyst, or else the analyst's therapeutic influence will falter. This means that the analyst must maintain his neutrality toward the patient's associations, not toward the patient.

The emotional intimacy in the therapeutic collaboration imposes a demand on the patient that mobilizes his capacity for sublimated love. The analyst must respond with sufficient tact and understanding so that it remains a positive force in the therapeutic process. It is a common analytic observation that the frustrations of childhood have the meaning to the patient that his love is worthless or evil, and therefore that *he* is worthless or evil. Subtle reinforcements of this fantasy can occur as much from tactless silences as from premature interpretations when the patient is struggling with conflicts surrounding this issue in the transference. The necessity for appropriately timed interpretations by the analyst requires him to be receptive to the patient's love, regardless of the gratifications to the patient that this implies.

This principle can be demonstrated clearly in the vicissitudes of a severe borderline psychotic patient's tenuous grasp on object relations in the transference. Although she was not treated entirely by conventional analytic techniques, her severe psychopathology permits a dramatic demonstration of this issue. This twenty-eight-year-old woman suffered from life-threatening anorexia nervosa and dysphagia, as well as severe migraine.

An intensely ambivalent transference developed early in the treatment. The patient expressed overt demands that I have sexual relations with her and insisted that she would kill herself if I refused. As it became clear to her that her threats of suicide would not move me, her rage and hatred became extremely intense. They seemed to reach a peak during one session while she was expressing her hatred of me. She paused and then described the onset of scotomata; these were characteristic of the prodromal stage of her migraine attacks. I said, "When you hate me like this, you forget that you love me."

The scotomata stopped abruptly, and the patient did not have a migraine attack. She became much calmer, and this appeared to be a turning point in her treatment. Her emerging capacity to sustain a positive attachment through the vicissitudes of her ambivalent struggles subsequently permitted some working through of transference conflicts involving primitive cannibalistic fantasies. She acknowledged that her sexual desire was to suck my penis, rather than for coitus. She "discovered," spontaneously, that her dysphagia was "caused" by the fantasy that my penis was stuck in her throat. This was followed by the relief of that symptom; and the next visit she "discovered," again spontaneously, that her anorexia was caused by a feeling of fullness related to the fantasy that she had swallowed my penis. Although some of her childlike qualities were not entirely resolved by the treatment, which continued for some time, her long-standing symptoms of anorexia and dysphagia were substantially relieved, and her migraine episodes stopped. (An unexpected follow-up, fifteen years later, revealed that the symptoms had not recurred during that time.)

Psychoanalysts are taught well to avoid being seduced by their patients' transference love and to recognize its displacement from childhood objects. Reaction formations against this seductive influence, however, must also be guarded against. Otherwise, the fact might be overlooked that this predominantly nonerotic love is identical to that which is a requirement in all emotionally charged relationships, including the analytic relationship. It is thereby helped to survive the inevitable neurotic incursions and to become more firmly stabilized in the course of working through the transference neurosis. The result of successful analysis is not that the patient loves the analyst less, but that the love becomes less ambivalent, so that the normal mourning process at the end of analysis can be successful.

Technique

The patient's earliest anxieties in the analytic setting and his efforts to cope with them commonly reveal a myriad of obstructions to the establishment of the basic transference and preclude an attitude of passivity or silence by the analyst. Not only the direct associations to the analytic setting and the analyst, but the rhythm of associations and pauses in their flow, the affective responses, both appropriate and inappropriate, as well as their absence, all invite confrontations and preliminary interpretations in the context of the developing basic transference. At the same time, this permits the analyst to evaluate the patient's tolerance for anxiety and his character defenses, as well as his capacity to participate in the analytic investigation at that time. These events provide both the opportunities and the stimuli for the relatively conflict-free aspects of the patient's ego to become attached to the analyst—that is, to establish the basic transference.

Of course, issues related to the basic transference recur throughout the course of the analysis, and they must be worked over and worked through repeatedly. Likewise, the focus on the basic transference does not suggest that other issues are not dealt with analytically as they arise at the beginning of treatment. This includes especially formulations regarding regressive defenses against anxiety. I believe that this perspective does, however, help to formulate confrontations and interpretations in a manner that is most useful to the patient and the analysis.

Evidence of a patient's ability to develop such a sublimated therapeutic attachment is, in my experience, the most important factor determining prognosis. Manifestations of symptoms, however serious, are a statement of the therapeutic task; the capacity to participate with the kind of emotional rapport expressed by the basic transference is a statement of whether the therapeutic task can be accomplished. The existence of certain severe character disorders may, of course, make this issue—the problems associated with the development of the basic transference—the principle therapeutic focus for long periods of time. This includes especially the so-called narcissistic and borderline disorders. In the absence of the development of such an attachment, there may be unanalyzable psychopathology or unsuitability of the analyst for a particular patient.

Any delay in the development of the basic transference due to excessive silence by the analyst creates a danger of mobilizing or reinforcing the regressive defenses of the patient. In particular, the grandiose fantasies of the patient, along with the idealization of the analyst, may become major obstacles to effective analytic work. If these regressive fantasies are stimulated by the deprivations of the analytic setting before there is an effective therapeutic relationship, the possibility of successful analytic work is at least delayed, and it may become an insurmountable resistance. The misapplication of the rule of abstinence through excessive silence at the beginning of an analysis must carry this risk.

A patient who came to see me, over a year after he had terminated his first analysis, in all probability exemplified this problem. He described a remarkably idealized image of his first analyst, whom I knew to be an experienced clinician. The patient felt that he had, in turn, been highly admired by his analyst. The patient had interpreted his analyst's silences as evidence of recognition of the patient's unique capacity for self-analysis. The result was, he said, that he had completed his "self-analysis" according to both Freudian and Kleinian theories, consecutively. He thought that the deep depression that followed the termination was an indication of a need only for a small amount of additional treatment to "finish up."

In a short time my confrontations of manifestations of resistance mobilized intense anger and a predisposition to act out. He wanted to participate in psychological "encounter groups," and he tried to rationalize relatively frequent interruptions in the schedule. Finally, he acknowledged that he didn't believe in *any* psychoanalytic theory or analyst, but that he would try to work with me because of the painful depression that had been the original motivation for analytic treatment.

Iatrogenic deficiencies in the therapeutic environment are most readily tolerated by patients who like this one are preconditioned and begin analysis with a kind of religious zeal. Superficially they may be the most sophisticated and knowledgeable patients, and they often present a special resistance of idealization and grandiosity from the beginning of treatment. These resistances often derive from intensely narcissistic and masochistic character traits which present a serious challenge to the therapeutic process in any case. The usual criteria of validation of interpretations are obscured by the patient's idealization and uncritical acceptance of all analytic ideas, including the image of the silent analyst. The defensive nature of this kind of response must be recognized, along with the doubts and hostility that it masks, before analysis can be productive.

Early in an analysis, before an effective therapeutic collaboration has developed, confrontations regarding neurotic behavior outside the analytic setting, may present special problems, as with the patient just described. It is at this time that acting out is most likely to reflect resistances to the analytic treatment itself, rather than regressive displacements of emerging transference conflicts. This often needs to be interpreted quickly, before it intrudes on the development of the basic transference and jeopardizes the treatment. The patient, of course, may respond by creating the image of the analyst as a surrogate parent who forbids certain behavior. In other words, the interpretation of one resistance may mobilize another. This is not a contraindication to resistance interpretation involving acting out, but is an observation of what goes on during much analytic work. A simple confrontation, such as a statement that the patient's behavior is an attempt to relieve his problem in order to avoid its analysis, may at times be sufficient to discourage early acting out. At the very least, such a confrontation attempts to bring the behavior into the analysis. Avoidance or delay of such confrontations can lead to premature major decisions by the patient that interfere seriously with the evolution of the basic transference and inhibit development of the transference neurosis.

A patient in his second analysis demonstrated the serious consequences of this kind of error in his first analysis. He had sought analytic treatment because of a work inhibition that had prevented him from completing his thesis for his Ph.D. He had been involved with a woman he had considered marrying, and he said that he had talked about this with his first analyst. He married her shortly after the analysis began.

After three and a half years, external circumstances forced him to change analysts and he began treatment with me. By this time he had withdrawn from the Ph.D. program and had a job as a blue-collar worker. He described the current major issue in his analysis to be provocative behavior which repeatedly led to serious arguments with his wife. My direct questions regarding this behavior led the patient to "discover" that he had been very passive and submissive in the relationship, taking the blame unnecessarily for all their problems. As the defensive nature of this behavior became clear, the patient changed in his relationship with his wife, and a divorce appeared inevitable. Passive homosexual fantasies began to emerge in the transference and became available for analytic work. This material was also clearly related to the work inhibition that had brought him into analysis originally.

During the first analysis, not only had the marriage defended against unconscious homosexual fantasies, but it had inhibited the development of a therapeutic attachment that might have mobilized more active participation in the analytic process. In effect, the early acting out had represented a resistance to the analysis itself.

The Oral Triad and Transference

Having the patient recline on the couch contributes both to the development of the basic transference as well as to mobilizing conflicts associated with it. These conflicts are, inevitably, derivatives of the oral triad—that is, the wish to eat, the wish to be eaten, and the wish to sleep (Lewin, 1950). In this regard, Lewin (1955) remarked that "the couch is reminiscent of *sleep* and [is] therefore an important element of the nursing situation" (p. 179). According to Lewin, the analyst provides stimuli for symbolic sleep as well as for arousal.

Two clinical vignettes exemplify different aspects of this issue. A thirty-year-old male patient, in treatment because of psychic impotence, described early in the analysis a "dream about a dream." The manifest dream was that he awoke in the morning and his new car, which he had in fact recently purchased, wasn't there. He asked people about it, but they said he had never had a car. He went to the car dealer, and it turned out that he had only dreamed that he had a new car. An old car was there, and the salesman said that he could have it. His father said, "Take it. It's a good car. It's all I have now."

The patient liked to sleep a great deal, he said, because it allowed him to dream. The real world was too frustrating. His dreamworld was "all I have now," the vestige of his childhood with a physically cruel as well as overtly rejecting father. The manifest dream reflected the major resistance current in the analysis. He made the couch into a place to "sleep" and to "dream"—the new car, the analysis, and the real world were only a dream. These fantasies about the analysis had been emerging into consciousness at this time.

The patient generally avoided direct responses to my confrontations, but he revealed that he attempted secretly to build an image of me from my interpretations so that he could copy me in his quest for a "charismatic" identity with magical powers in business and personal relations.

Yet he continued his self-defeating, masochistic behavior outside the analysis.

Later on, he dreamed that I gave him instructions that allowed him to avoid his self-defeating behavior in his business. When he awoke, he "felt ready" to make use of the "instructions," and he began, gradually, to respond directly to my confrontations.

The patient demonstrated fairly clearly, I think, several problems that had their roots in the oral triad and delayed the establishment of the basic transference. At the time of the first dream, sleep represented a resistance and had to be treated as such. He used the couch as a place to sleep and dream, but it appeared that he had to play the role of both parent and infant, a fantasied dyadic relationship from which the analyst was excluded. Efforts to work through conflicts associated with later developmental stages could not be integrated by the patient's ego until some of the conflict associated with the basic transference was relieved and he could begin to respond directly to my confrontations. His efforts to incorporate psychically my idealized image in order to become a "charismatic" person represented a derivative of orality that could not stimulate the analytic work to become an integrative experience.

In the second dream, the analyst's image had become sufficiently integrated by the patient so that it could be made into an element of his dreamworld. It had become a part of the sleep fantasy, and the patient was ready to be aroused by the analyst from the narcissistic regression. A significant step had been made in the development of the basic transference.

The contrasting transference responses demonstrate some important features regarding the therapeutic process. The "narcissistic" withdrawal at the time of the first dream was not psychotic—in the sense of withdrawal of "object cathexis" (Freud, 1914b). The image of his mother was in his fantasied sleep on the couch, but he had to play both roles. Later, as a development of the initial rapport that had helped to initiate the treatment, I had, to a limited extent, replaced the gratifying mother whom he had loved. The creative aspects of this latter state derived from memories of the gratifying parent and led to productive use of the analytic situation. The "sleep" was no longer entirely a manifestation of resistance. That is, to the extent that the analyst was a representation of the frustrating parent out of the past, who had nothing to offer but frustration, the resistance was dominant. As the analyst's image became stabilized as a representation of memories of gratification, the basic transference evolved and provided the foundation for further emotional growth.

Another patient, described previously in chapter 4, demonstrated dramatically the emergence from a severe regression that also had its roots in the oral triad. The patient had been seriously involved in drugs—especially intravenous use of cocaine—prostitution, and a check-forgery ring.

During the first year of analysis the patient participated in dangerous and erratic but no longer illegal behavior. After a little over a year, the patient emerged abruptly into a symptom neurosis with moderate to severe depressive symptoms. This change was initiated by her sudden "discovery," based on an earlier confrontation, that it was possible to "think" before she acted, and to consider the consequences of her behavior. This change was also heralded by a dream: She had found a hungry puppy in front of a movie. She picked it up and rushed home to feed it, and it ate an enormous amount. She was happy watching it eat, and she knew that it was going to get better.

Her associations to the dream led her to acknowledge her "hunger for love," which she had previously been unaware of, and which she said was now directed toward me.

Following this hour, the patient repeatedly experienced a state of sleepy relaxation on the couch. She felt as if she were going to sleep, although she did not actually do so. The experience represented to her a state of "total submission," not unlike that which she had formerly experienced in her submission to her procurer. When she had experienced it with him, however, it had stimulated intense anxiety, which was relieved by erratic and impulsive behavior. Now it was not accompanied by anxiety but led instead to productive use of the analytic dialogue. The conflicts associated with the oral triad had evidently been mastered sufficiently so that its derivatives could lead to integrative therapeutic experiences, which included the analysis of conflicts associated with later developmental stages. It appeared as if the analyst had become, like the mother of early childhood, an extension of the patient's ego, and he could provide the foundation for the resumption of the ego's growth. She could begin to participate in the analysis in the manner described by Lewin (1954): "The analysand is in a quasi dream, making accessible to consciousness (which is the manifest analytic picture) memory traces from all parts of the psychic apparatus, even those near its topographical and chronological beginning" (p. 509).

This therapeutic transformation demonstrated the primitive roots of the basic transference in her addictive and behavioral symptoms, and their development into the kind of "therapeutic addiction" that is commonly observed during productive periods of analytic work.

Is there an apparent contradiction regarding the analysis of oral conflict before the basic transference has been established? The answer is that this is not an all-or-none proposition. The patient must be allowed to function in a manner that is consistent with his level of neurotic regression. That is, he is allowed to sleep and to dream, symbolically, and to achieve the nurturing of the precarious healthy portion of his personality that stimulates the beginning of the basic attachment. The analyst's silence while he listens must be accompanied by empathic understanding of the patient's mature desire to get well, as well as by an understanding of the nature and intensity of his suffering. The silent listening should be maintained only so long as it is productive in this context. Otherwise the patient's anxiety leads instead to reinforcement of the regressive defenses that can inhibit a stable basic attachment. The analyst cannot force the patient to be aroused from his sleep-dream regression with deeper interpretations until the analyst's influence—that derived from the basic attachment—has reached a substantial level. Coldness or detachment from the analyst, including that manifested by inappropriate silence, disturbs this development.

The relationship of the basic transference with the oral triad leads to the question of whether it should be considered a regressive phenomenon, or at least "regression in the service of the ego" (Kris, 1952). I agree with Greenacre (1968) that "such a need for relationship is not in itself necessarily regressive, since it is . . . a necessary component in all . . . productive activities in life" (p. 212). The relatively conflict-free derivatives of the oral triad, including the sleeplike state sometimes observed during the most productive phases of analysis, represent a mature psychological process with creative potential. It is a manifestation of the growing capacity to experience mature derivatives of merging fantasies without excessive anxiety, and it is accompanied by a firm capacity for reality testing and delay of discharge. When it is mobilized in the transference it represents a progression toward a mature, trusting relationship in which the childhood conflicts may be reexperienced as memories, rather than as regressive phenomena operating as resistances.

In this regard, Lewin (1955) commented as follows: "it rather looks as though we [psychoanalysts] may have some resistance to the idea that analytic therapy and technique are related to sleep" (p. 500). The analyst's silence is part of the total gestalt participating in the patient's fantasy of sleep on the couch. The silence has been acknowledged as a means of frustrating the patient, but analysts have continued to resist acknowledging the full implications of its role as a means of gratifying him in a sleep-breast merger relationship.

The Self Psychology of Kohut

Kohut's work is pertinent to my thesis, not only because it deals with some of the clinical issues that I have addressed in regard to the basic transference but also because of his excellent observations of a group of transference phenomena which he has organized in his psychology of the self. Furthermore, his approach has evidently yielded some positive therapeutic results with a difficult group of patients. Gedo (1980), although critical of significant aspects of the clinical reports in Goldberg's casebook (1978) of patients treated according to Kohut's theoretical orientation, acknowledged substantial improvements in the patients' tolerance of anxiety and increased stability in their lives. Regardless of whether Kohut's approach is consistent with a traditional definition of psychoanalytic treatment, his views need to be given serious consideration.

Kohut (1971) and Kohut and Wolf (1978) described a group of patients manifesting specific transference phenomena suggesting a failure in self-object differentiation, but who appeared to be so well integrated in their character defenses that there was no evidence of psychotic or borderline disorder:

The narcissistic transferences which are pathogno-
monic for these syndromes were subdivided into two
types: (1) the *mirror transference* in which an insufficiently
or faultily responded to childhood need for a source of
accepting-confirming "mirroring" is revived in the treatment situation, and (2) the *idealizing transference* in which
a need for merger with a source of "idealized" strength
and calmness is similarly revived. . . . it became clear that
the essence of the disturbance from which these patients
suffered could not be adequately explained within the
framework of classical drive-and-defense psychology.
[Kohut and Wolf, pp. 413–414]

It appears to me that Kohut foundered on the same
problems of gratification and frustration that I have been
discussing, and that this may have prevented him from
integrating his clinical observations with the conflict theory
of neurosis. Kohut (1971) said, in regard to the therapeutic
setting, "The relative stability of this narcissistic transference amalgamation, however, is the prerequisite for the
performance of the analytic task (the systematic process of
working through) in the pathogenic narcissistic areas of
the personality" (p. 32); and, "From the sought-for object,
however, (i.e., the analyst), the analysand expects the performance of certain basic functions in the realm of narcissistic homeostasis which his own psyche is unable to
provide" (p. 47).

Kohut made it explicitly clear that the analyst must
provide this contribution to the "narcissistic homeostasis"
by means of an "empathic bridge." Yet, Kohut denied the
significance of this as gratification. He said that, after mobilizing the infantile wish,

The analytic process (a) prevents the satisfaction of
the childhood wish on the infantile level (optimal frustration; analytic abstinence); it consistently counteracts

(through interpretations) the regressive evasion of the
infantile wish or need. . . . Being thus, on the one hand,
continuously reactivated without being gratified and, on
the other, prevented from regressive escape, only one
way remains open to the infantile drive, wish, or need. . . .
In other words, the analytic process attempts to keep the
infantile need activated while simultaneously cutting off
all roads except the one toward maturation and realistic
employment. [p. 197]

On the other hand, Ornstein (1974), in a footnote to
his summary of Kohut's approach, clearly focused on the
issue of gratification and frustration, but without offering
any resolution. He expressed the view that the gratifications to the patient that were offered by the analyst on a
sublimated level satisfied the narcissistic strivings of the
patient and provided a crucial healing influence. "To dis-
pel any misunderstanding," he wrote,

it should be stressed that in the analytic process described
by Kohut, there is no wish fulfillment other than the
empathic understanding communicated by the analyst.
This wish fulfillment is a sublimated antidote to the experiences of a nonempathic, traumatizing childhood environment. This minimum of wish fulfillment, however,
Kohut feels occurs in any properly conducted analysis.
[p. 140]

While he recognized the importance of the sublimated
gratifications from the analyst as an essential ingredient
in the resumption of emotional growth, Ornstein described
this as gratifying unresolved infantile needs. This failed
to take into account the inevitable development of the patient's sublimated love for the analyst and its therapeutic
significance. It also prevented him from considering adequately the "compulsion to repeat" as a clinical concept.

In his struggle with what appears to be a basic inner contradiction, Kohut (1971) said,

> The specific attribute of the analytic situation which allows, and encourages, the emergence of the pathological self is the following. In its central aspects the analytic situation is *not real*, in the usual sense of the word. It has a specific reality which resembles to a certain extent the reality of the artistic experience, such as that of the theater. [p. 210; italics mine]

This statement supports a resistance position seen in many patients—that their feelings in the analytic situation are "not real." This stands in contrast, however, to the implications of Kohut's technical recommendation that the analyst be "empathic" and "understanding," a therapeutic stance designed to stimulate the patient's responses to a real, contemporary person, the analyst. These gratifications stimulate the patient's sublimated (nonerotic) love for the analyst, and the latter must respond to this with due respect. Kohut denied the nature as well as the significance of this attachment to the analyst. The result was that, while acknowledging the inevitability of establishing rapport with the patient, Kohut (1971) concluded that "to assign to the patient's nonspecific, nontransference rapport with the analyst a position of primary significance in the analysis of these forms of psychopathology would, . . . in my opinion, be erroneous" (p. 31).

The result was a theoretical dilemma which Kohut attempted to resolve with a loosely knit metapsychological structure involving "narcissistic libido," which was defined in large part by the object of its cathexis. This redefined the nature of the patient's attachment to the analyst and brought Kohut's formulations into juxtaposition with traditional conflict theory. Paradoxically, in his construction of the roots of "narcissistic transference" phenomena, Kohut described a *defensive* constellation. "The equilibrium of primary narcissism," he wrote, "is disturbed by the unavoidable shortcomings of maternal care, but the child replaces the previous perfection (a) by establishing a grandiose and exhibitionistic image of the self . . . and (b) by giving over the previous perfection to an admired, omnipotent (transitional) self-object . . ." (p. 25). That is, he held that the narcissism that he observed had its roots in responses to tension-anxiety associated with the loss of a state of pleasure, the "perfection" of the primary unity with the mother. This parallels Freud's description (1926) of the infant's response to the trauma of a "loss of object," the first "danger situation" among the events leading to anxiety and defense.

The narcissistic transferences described by Kohut and their resolution can, in fact, be fully explained within the framework of defense and conflict theory. This depends upon our understanding of oral conflict, especially in regard to Lewin's oral triad. Conflicts in this area predispose patients to difficulties in sustaining stable attachments during all subsequent developmental stages; they contribute to the kind of narcissistic compromises described by Kohut and lead to the sense of isolation and emotional deadness observed in that large group of patients. Kohut described a nurturing (empathic) approach that contributes to the patient's symbolic sleep. The associations represent the manifest dream, as Lewin described, and the narcissistic transferences parallel the primary wish-fulfillments of dreams—that is, the grandiosity and merger fantasies.

If the patient has enough capacity to mobilize a sustained attachment to the analyst in this nurturing climate, it can provide the foundation for the resumption of emotional growth. The patient's contribution to the sublimated attachment provides the catalyst for his emotional growth out of the compulsion to repeat his narcissistic "transferences." Some patients have significant levels of conflict that interferes with their development of this sublimated attachment—the basic transference—and that issue takes up a significant part of the treatment.

Kohut, I think, also classified his narcissistic patients on the bases of faulty clinical criteria. Goldberg (1978) summarized the clinical bases of the observations in this way: "If one undermines the defensive narcissistic position in a classical 'transference' neurosis, the nuclear oedipal conflict will emerge; the same intervention in a case in which the narcissistic phenomena are not defensive, but are manifestations of a narcissistic personality disorder sets in motion a regression and break-up of the cohesive self" (p. 5).

That kind of regression is more likely to occur as the result of premature interpretations of essential narcissistic defenses, especially if the basic transference is not firmly established. Premature interpretations of any defensive constellation, in fact, carry the danger of inducing pathological regressions. It is also true that, in some patients, the premature interpretation of narcissistic defenses leads to the emergence of oedipal material that defends against the primitive ambivalence associated with the narcissistic position.

A brief clinical vignette will demonstrate some of these principles. A research scientist had asked for treatment because of chronic depression and intense feelings of inferiority. Fairly early, he began to recognize the grandiosity that existed behind his feelings of inferiority, and a "mirror transference" began to emerge. He believed that only he understood the high levels that could be reached, and that his protestations of inferiority were simultaneously assertions of knowing more than anyone else. When I made an interpretation, he either avoided any direct response to what I said and went on with his previous associations, or protested angrily that he was trying to explain something to me. Finally, he recognized the fantasy that when I became convinced of his superiority I would see to it that he received what was coming to him, an ideal existence without frustration—"the big tit," he said.

During a "good hour," a number of issues began to come together. He acknowledged the embarrassment at seeing his name on a paper he had published. He was ashamed of its importance to him and the satisfaction it gave him, and he recognized that his protestations of the inferiority of the product defended him against the feeling of shame. He then complained of his inability to put all the contradictory elements together, and then he recalled his obstinacy in refusing a pleasant experience when he was a child. He recognized, then, his obstinacy in refusing to make the analytic insights a part of himself.

The patient paused and then said that he felt like going to sleep. Then he protested that this was a means of escaping an important topic. I said that he wanted to relax, to associate, and to allow me to be the analyst, but was afraid I would abandon him as his parents had done. This was followed by associations about his anger, the loss of control with his son, and the fright that he had seen on his son's face. Then he recalled how angry he had been at me, on occasion, and how destructive he felt his anger could be.

This report demonstrates the defensive nature of the narcissistic transference of this patient, while he symbolically expressed his hostile rejection and destruction of the analyst in his grandiose fantasies. The sleepy relaxation heralded a significant development of the basic transference; after a brief encounter with his separation anxiety, associations followed regarding destructive fantasies which had been defended against. These now began to occupy a more conspicuous role in the treatment.

On a purely descriptive level, the neurotic manifestations of narcissism—i.e., of self-centeredness—are the opposite of object relatedness, regardless of their dynamic roots. The latter is manifested by the capacity for empathy, in which the qualities of objects are observed and responded to without excessive anxiety. This capacity derives primarily from conflict-free derivatives of the oral triad. In that context, the patients discussed by Kohut could be described as having disorders of the capacity for empathy.

Some capacity for empathy with the analyst, however, is the basis of the patient's ability to respond to the requirements of the psychoanalytic situation and to develop rapport with the analyst as a contemporary person. Furthermore, the continuing development of this capacity provides the primary criterion of clinical success—the evolution of the patient's capacity to respond with empathy in his personal relationships without excessive residual neurotic disturbances. Empathy has a contemporary quality and is flexible, whereas neurosis rigidly repeats infantile traumas. The stabilization of object relations, as well as the establishment of sublimations, needs to be observed in this context if psychoanalytic accomplishments are to be differentiated from those appropriate to other forms of psychotherapy.

The personal relationships that are initially observed in the narcissistic patients described by Kohut are accompanied by a sense of deadness, an affective state that reflects major inhibitions in feeling for others. Goldberg, in his introduction to the Kohutian casebook, noted the following: "To be sure, much of the content of the associative material in both categories of pathology is concerned with the oedipal drama, but persons with narcissistic personality disorders use these interactions to attain a feeling of life and vitality, and such conflict is thus a secondary matter in their pathology" (p. 5).

My own observations indicate that a patient does not begin to "feel alive" simply because of an improvement in self-esteem, as Kohut's theory of narcissism suggests, unless such improvement is a consequence of the development of a capacity for more mature and positive object-related affects, including empathy. I have repeatedly observed a transition to "feeling alive" as a result of developments in the transference: when the patient begins to develop positive feelings for me, trust in a human relationship begins to evolve. The capacity for empathy is the factor determining whether there can be satisfaction in all personal relationships. Among patients with narcissistic transferences and feelings of deadness, primitive conflicts associated with merger fantasies and narcissistic detachment are commonly observed, but other areas of disturbance also contribute to this affective state.

Rothstein (1980) described what appear to be failures in the resolution of neurotic transference reactions in Goldberg's casebook. Rothstein's most significant criticism is of the self psychologists' failure to confront the sadomasochistic derivatives of archaic conflicts that have been observed with great regularity in association with narcissistic defenses, and which contribute significantly to the affective deadness of these patients. It must be acknowledged, of course, that Kohut (1971) recognized the clinical necessity of dealing with the function of idealization as a defense against hostility. He referred to the "defensive use of idealization, i.e., of (over)idealizations which . . . buttress secondarily . . . denials of a structurally deeper lying hostility" (p. 75).

It appears, however, that Kohut's approach deals with anger that is secondary to the frustrations of the defensive constellations, but not with the ambivalence that is primarily defended against. The case reports demonstrate that Kohut's theoretical formulations can be utilized in the service of the analyst's counterresistances against dealing with primitive aggression. The internal contradictions in the theory make it suited to such abuse; and the basic premise on which it rests, that conflict theory fails to comprehend his observations, is not true.

Kohut hypothesized that a primary function of the parent is to provide support for and reinforcement of an evolving self-esteem. The alternative view suggests that gratification of the primary needs of the infant stimulates the origins of object-love, and that this provides the more important basis of evolving self-esteem. This is much more than a philosophical or metapsychological issue. In the clinical situation, in the context of the developing therapeutic attachment, do we focus primarily on resistances to the sublimated attachment to (love for) the analyst, or do we concern ourselves with direct reinforcements of the patient's self-esteem? Furthermore, in the later stages of treatment, is the integration of the analyst's role into the ego based largely on memories of sublimated gratifications *from* the analyst, or is it the result of the development of relatively conflict-free sublimated affection *for* the analyst? I believe that there is ample clinical evidence that the resolution of ambivalent conflict that intrudes on the basic transference creates the situation for the integration of the image and role of the analyst and permits the patient to leave him.

The improved functioning of the patients treated in accordance with Kohut's theories, along with their increased tolerance of anxiety, can be understood on the basis of two therapeutic elements. The empathy and understanding provided by the analyst, which help reinforce the latent healthy portions of the patients' personalities, provide a stabilizing influence for any patient who can respond to it, and regularly permit increased tolerance of anxiety. The second element is the modification of defenses against hostility based on insight, primarily on a contemporary basis. This is an effective psychotherapeutic constellation, one that permits significant reorganization of defenses with substantial decrease in the intensity of faulty superego responses. Such clinical results should not be regarded lightly, especially when dealing with very severe psychopathology. In all probability, many of the partial successes of traditional psychoanalytic treatment in alleviating symptoms rely principally on just this constellation of factors. Such clinical improvements do not, however, justify revisions of psychoanalytic technique or theory.

It is a profound paradox to me that both Macalpine and Kohut advocated the mobilization of regression to an infantile level of frustration, and that this was supposed to establish the condition for the resumption of emotional growth. Macalpine attempted to achieve this situation by means of frustrating silence; Kohut by providing empathic understanding of the regressed fantasies while maintaining the atmosphere of frustration. Both advocated a process of "working through" which relied heavily on a therapeutic stance. Both also acknowledged the necessity for the existence of rapport between patient and analyst in order to get the treatment under way, and neither permitted that essential clinical observation to become a part of their theories of the therapeutic process.

It appears to me that excessive concern with the issue of infantile gratification of the patient has intruded seriously upon the evolution of psychoanalytic theory and technique. Patients are unable to receive satisfaction of their infantile needs; that is why they come for treatment. The frustrations of their infantile needs contribute the major share of the pain of their neurotic symptoms. In focusing on patients with manifestations of narcissism, it must be remembered that we are dealing with a group of patients that have in common severe depressive symptoms, and it is this painful symptom that demands special attention and understanding. I see no rationale clinically arrived at for disagreeing with Freud's view (1915a) with regard to infantile gratifications: "And what we could offer would never be anything else than a surrogate, for the patient's condition is such that, until her repressions [defenses] are removed, she is incapable of getting real satisfaction" (p. 165).

Kohut has been credited by Rothstein (1980) with the recognition and management of countertransference problems associated with treating narcissistic transferences. For example, Kohut (1971) wrote,

> The analyst's own narcissistic needs, however, may make it difficult for him to tolerate a situation in which he is reduced to the seemingly passive role of being the mirror of the patient's infantile narcissism, and he may, therefore, subtly or openly, through gross parapraxes and symptomatic acts or through rationalized and theoretically buttressed behavior, interfere with the establishment or the maintenance of the mirror transference. [p. 272]

This clinical situation demands great patience from the analyst, at the very least. On the other hand, I wonder how often the analyst's countertransference problems are the result of feelings of boredom, helplessness, and impatience as a result of misguided passive attitudes of silently frustrating the patient in order to permit the development of a theoretically determined regression; and whether this might be less a problem, and the analyst more comfortably empathic, if he felt free to interact with the patient in order to help the patient to develop a therapeutic attachment, as well as to recognize the defensive nature of his neurotic transference responses.

Transference and Countertransference Implications

Does the analyst's "freely suspended attention" mobilize an affective state in him that parallels that of the patient's symbolic sleep on the couch described by Lewin? And does this stimulate an attachment to the patient, with its roots in the analyst's mother-infant bond, that intensifies his feelings for, and attachment to, the patient, with all the neurotic—and real—dangers of disappointment, and with all the demands for narcissistic defenses? The analyst's empathic interest in the patient has the same dynamic roots as the patient's sublimated responses to the analyst. It must be sustained with intense self-discipline over a number of years in order to elicit the responses from the healthy portion of the patient. This reciprocal attachment provides the sine qua non of psychoanalytic treatment.

I think that some of the difficulties in understanding the roles of gratification and frustration in this alliance may be demonstrated by an examination of the paradoxical use of the term *object* relations. If the more appropriate term *personal* relations were substituted, we would be much closer to what we are talking about. But then we would encounter the taboo of countertransference. When the personal relationship that the analyst offers his patients is considered, and especially the gratifications offered to his patients in these personal relationships, we are forced to acknowledge that the therapeutic situation has emotional significance for ourselves, the analysts. Ego gratifications are provided, not only in the work but in the relationship with patients, which is the converse of the ego gratifications accruing to patients via the sublimated transference. It may be that these gratifications are the essential ingredients that make it possible for the analyst to accept comfortably the inevitable frustrations of his work. When we refer to patients we like, there can still be the defensive attitude of hiding behind the professional status of doctors with patients, rather than acknowledging that we offer ourselves as persons, not objects, for transferences; and only insofar as each patient is able to establish rapport with this person as a contemporary is the analysis able to proceed. These potential gratifications to the analyst are the very bases of neurotic countertransferences, but do not in themselves constitute disturbances of the analytic situation. This aspect of the personal relationship—that which is free of neurotic determinants—is an essential ingredient in the therapeutic atmosphere. Both the therapeutic process in analysis and the theoretical constructions of the therapeutic process must fail if this aspect of treatment is neglected.

Conversely, the attachment of the patient to the analyst, both in the basic transference as well as the neurotic responses, must be used for the investigative goals of the treatment exclusively. Any effort to gratify inappropriate or infantile needs for the patient are not only certain to fail, but they inevitably must distort the therapeutic relationship and doom the treatment. The analyst must achieve satisfaction in his task, but he will impair the analytic process if he permits anything to intrude upon the analytic goal of making the unconscious conscious. While this aspect of the technique of psychoanalysis must be differentiated from the total therapeutic process, it is imperative to recognize that the analyst's integrity in sustaining the analytic atmosphere of investigation is an absolute requirement that enables the therapeutic process to proceed. The analysis as an investigation provides the foundation for the analyst's expression of his empathic interest in the patient which mobilizes the basic transference, as well as for the crucial discoveries that the neurotic conflicts belong to the past.

The analyst may not be able to exceed the limits of his own maturity and understanding of human behavior in his work with his patients. It is possible, however, to offer less. A mask of impersonal objectivity is just that, a mask that contributes to an unreal atmosphere and contaminates the patient's transference responses much more than the relaxed offering of the analyst's personality in his style of working. The respect for human dignity and the achievement of mature emotional gratification in personal relationships must be of primary importance to the analyst, rather than the goal of making the unconscious conscious. The latter is a technique, a means of achieving the former.

7

Summing Up

1. The two primary psychological experiences are pleasure and frustration. Infantile and childhood gratifications result in modifications of the inborn needs, or drives, that promote their adaptations to adult functions. Instinctual derivatives that have undergone development as a result of such gratifications must be renewed by further gratifications appropriate to their developmental level. This is summarized in the term "cycle of satisfaction." This sequence is essential for the achievement of increasing levels of maturity, stability, and flexibility. That is, children need to be stimulated to function at their appropriate developmental levels, so that those psychological functions which have evolved can be reinforced and helped to mature. Frustrations contribute to emotional growth to the extent that such renewals of the drive derivatives are stimulated; otherwise they inhibit psychological development and provoke intrapsychic conflicts.

2. The therapeutic process in psychoanalysis demonstrates certain phenomena that parallel childhood development. The initial gratifications of the therapeutic relationship provide the basis of rapport so that the conflict-free core of the patient is mobilized for the basic transference. Gratifications to the patient in the analytic setting are, therefore, essential to stimulate the therapeutic process in psychoanalysis, as are gratifications to the child that stim-

ulate emotional growth. These are an inevitable consequence of the therapeutic relationship, although such
gratifications must be restricted by the analyst to those that
are appropriate to the specific investigative goals. The analyst's manifestations of sincere therapeutic interest, his
empathic and appropriate responses, and his commitment
to the therapeutic process provide these gratifications,
though within the limits of the patient's capacity to respond
at a given time. The gratifications help stabilize the conflict-
free aspects of the patient's ego and provide an essential
catalyst for the resolution of neurotic conflict. Conversely,
both insufficient and inappropriate gratifications interfere
with childhood development and the therapeutic process.

3. Neurotic conflicts intrude on the therapeutic relationship from two sources. First, disturbances in the patient's
ability to participate in a stable interpersonal relationship,
as expressed in the basic positive transference, are generally due to conflicts associated with the oral triad (Lewin).
Second, intrusions may stem from conflicts associated with
later developmental stages.

4. The repetition of neurotic conflicts in the presence of
a stable, conflict-free positive transference constitutes the
transference neurosis. The establishment of the transference neurosis and the resultant insight provide access to
consciousness of previously repressed or otherwise de-
fended-against impulses. Once this is achieved the reintegration of infantile impulses becomes possible as a
consequence of their association with gratification. While
the development of insight is essential to this process, it is
not ordinarily sufficient, in itself, for a lasting therapeutic
effect. The process of working through requires first, the
establishment of the stable therapeutic relationship or positive transference, and then the repeated experience by

the patient of the childhood frustrations in the relatively gratifying environment made possible by the positive transference. Resolution of conflict inevitably leads to modifications of infantile needs, which become directed toward adult interests with the potential for greater satisfaction.

5. Observations of both childhood development and the therapeutic process support the validity of the proposed theory of consciousness. Satisfaction is conceptualized as an intrapsychic process, with conscious manifestations. This is translated into a metapsychological abstraction as discharge into consciousness. These two concepts, the cycle of satisfaction and discharge into consciousness, describe the pleasure principle. With the aid of these perspectives the apparent contradictions to the pleasure principle are resolved, and a universal principle of human behavior is defined.

6. Two classes of observation demonstrate the necessity for conceptualizing an aggressive drive with the capacity for hostile and destructive expression: frustrations of libidinal needs or their derivatives result in hostile responses; conversely, the subordination of aggression to libidinal goals is demonstrated in both sublimations and overt sexuality. Neurosis and destructive behavior both demonstrate inadequate subordination of aggressive drive derivatives to libidinal needs. In analytic treatment, the goal of subordinating and neutralizing the aggressive impulses that have carried infantile and destructive qualities is an essential aspect of the therapeutic process. Such observations suggest a supplement to the pleasure principle: The earliest libidinal satisfactions that initiate the cycle of satisfaction result in subordination of the accompanying aggressive drive components to libidinal goals. The asso-

ciated memories of libidinal satisfaction provide a basis for the development of lasting substructures that become organized into the ego. This process and its renewal through the cycle of satisfaction contribute to the flexibility that is essential for adult sublimated behavior as well as for sexual discharge. Likewise, it maintains the synergistic functions of aggressive and libidinal drive derivatives in the pursuit of satisfaction. These reconstructions provide an additional biological perspective to psychoanalytic theory by means of their integration with Lorenz's studies in ethology.

7. Memories of satisfaction that are associated with significant persons establish the basis for identifications contributing to the mature adult personality. Early frustrations lead to disturbances in the roots of the ego, the primary identifications. Later frustrations lead to conflicts that are manifested by pathological superego formations and other ambivalent identifications. The therapeutic process in psychoanalysis results in the replacement of ambivalent identifications with relatively nonambivalent ones that include aspects of the analytic experience.

8. Shame is associated with early disturbances related to the oral triad and object constancy. Guilt derives from later conflicts associated with a more intact ego, particularly oedipal conflicts. Depression is associated with the loss of an "ambivalent object." Conflicts associated with object-loss can be substantially overcome if the ambivalence is not excessive, but the process requires stable memories of satisfaction. Such stable memory systems are not firmly established in early childhood, regardless of the degree of ambivalence, with the result that real or fantasied losses are not effectively mourned. Disturbances of early attach-

ments consequently result in the predisposition to recurrent depressive reactions.

9. The three viewpoints of metapsychology can be integrated within this framework without the internal contradictions that have plagued the economic viewpoint:

(a) The drives represent the impulses of clinical observation. Libido is a unifying force that has an "object-seeking" quality. The aggressive drive may be destructive in its aims unless subordinated to libidinal goals. The libidinal and aggressive drives are modified by libidinal satisfactions that stimulate their development to more mature manifestations. In the absence of excessive conflict the drive derivatives operate synergistically in the pursuit of satisfying libidinal goals. Drive derivatives that become associated with excessive frustration release destructive impulses and stimulate neurotic compromises. Libidinal drives that fail to achieve early satisfaction are probably unavailable for later development.

(b) Ego structure derives from the organization of drive derivatives around memory systems associated with satisfaction. In order to establish and maintain their structural integrity, that is, their stability in the face of frustration and delay, they must be reinforced by the cycle of satisfaction. The superego is a substructure associated with oedipal frustrations in relatively stable relationships. If object relationships and the associated substructures are not stabilized, shame is more likely than guilt.

(c) The economic viewpoint is described by the pleasure principle, that is, the theory of consciousness and the cycle of satisfaction.

10. Normality and psychopathology may also be contrasted more effectively according to these criteria:

(a) The repetition compulsion reflects the persistent

demands of frustrated infantile needs. They influence behavior in the pursuit of satisfaction, but inevitably end in failure. The contrasting normal behavior involves the pursuit of satisfaction of adult drive derivatives and increasing levels of success related to the operation of the cycle of satisfaction; failures result in positive learning experiences.

(b) Frustrated infantile demands cannot be satisfied by adult experiences, with the result that their participation in both sublimated and sexual activities carries an aura of dissatisfaction. This is not relieved by further efforts, and affective responses may become increasingly focused on frustration and defense. "Normality" carries a quality of satisfaction in both sublimated pursuits as well as sexuality.

(c) Extremely hostile responses to frustration, or intense defenses against them, are prominent in psychopathology. In that case neither sublimation nor sexuality demonstrate adequate subordination of aggression to libidinal interests, with the result that there is either gross inhibition of activities that are identified with aggression, or, alternatively, the expression of cruel and sadistic impulses and behavior.

(d) The capacity for stable attachment bonds is a sine qua non of "normality." The tension affects—anxiety, shame, guilt, and depression—reflect the residues of infantile frustrations that intrude on stable attachment bonds. Disruptive influences may, however, be masked by narcissistic object choices, either by the kind of self-love that is exemplified by certain aspects of homosexuality, or in the pursuit of idealized properties in the object that provoke the additional danger of hostile envy.

References

Anthony, E.J. (1981), Guilt and the feminine self in psychoanalysis. In: *Object and Self: A Developmental Approach*, ed. S. Tuttman, C. Kaye, & M. Zimmerman. New York: International Universities Press.

Arlow, J. (1971), The dehumanization of psychoanalysis. Unpublished paper, summarized by R.C. Simmons, *Bull. Psychoanal. Assn. N.Y.*, 11:6–8.

Benedek, T. (1938), Adaptation to Reality in Early Infancy. *Psychoanal. Quart.*, 7:200–215.

Beres, D. (1966), Superego and depression. In: *Psychoanalysis: A General Psychology*, ed. R.M. Loewenstein. New York: International Universities Press.

Berliner, B. (1958), The role of object relations in moral masochism. *Psychoanal. Quart.*, 27:38–56.

Blum, H.P. (1978), Symbolic process and symbol formation. *Internat. J. Psycho-Anal.*, 59:455–472.

—— (1982), Theories of the self and psychoanalytic concepts: Discussion. *J. Amer. Psychoanal. Assn.*, 30:959–978.

Brenner, C. (1974), On the nature and development of affects: A unified theory. *Psychoanal. Quart.*, 43:532–556.

—— (1975), Affect and psychic conflict. *Psychoanal. Quart.*, 44:5–28.

Darwin, C. (1872), *The Expression of the Emotions in Man and Animals*. Chicago: University of Chicago Press, 1965.

Erikson, E.H. (1959), *Identity and the Life Cycle*. Psychological Issues, Monograph 1. New York: International Universities Press.

Evans, R.I. (1975), *Konrad Lorenz: The Man and His Ideas*. New York: Harcourt Brace Jovanovich.

Fenichel, O. (1941), *Problems of Psychoanalytic Technique*. New York: International Universities Press.

—— (1945), *The Psychoanalytic Theory of Neurosis*. New York: Norton.

Fleming, J. (1972), Early object deprivation and transference phenomena: The working alliance. *Psychoanal. Quart.*, 41:23–49.

Freud, A. (1949), Aggression: normal and pathological. *The Psychoanalytic Study of the Child*, 3/4:37–42. New York: International Universities Press.

Freud, S. (1900), The interpretations of dreams. *Standard Edition*, 4 & 5. London: Hogarth Press, 1953.

—— (1905), Three essays on the theory of sexuality. *Standard Edition*, 7:130–243. London: Hogarth Press, 1953.

—— (1911), Formulations on the two principles of mental functioning. *Standard Edition*, 12:218–226. London: Hogarth Press, 1958.

—— (1912a), The dynamics of transference. *Standard Edition*, 12:99–108. London: Hogarth Press, 1958.

—— (1912b), Recommendations to physicians practising psycho-analysis. *Standard Edition*, 12:111–120. London: Hogarth Press, 1958.

—— (1913), On beginning the treatment. *Standard Edition*, 12:123–144. London: Hogarth Press, 1958.

—— (1914a), Remembering, repeating and working through. *Standard Edition*, 12:147–156. London: Hogarth Press, 1958.

—— (1914b), On narcissism: An introduction. *Standard Edition*, 14:73–102. London: Hogarth Press, 1957.

—— (1915a), Observations on transference-love. *Standard Edition*, 12:159–171. London: Hogarth Press, 1958.

—— (1915b), Repression. *Standard Edition*, 14:146–158. London: Hogarth Press, 1958.

—— (1915c), The unconscious. *Standard Edition*, 14:166–215. London: Hogarth Press, 1957.

—— (1915d), Instincts and their vicissitudes. *Standard Edition*, 14:117–140. London: Hogarth Press, 1957.

—— (1916–1917), Introductory Lectures on Psycho-Analysis. *Standard Edition*, 15 & 16. London: Hogarth Press, 1963.

—— (1917), Mourning and melancholia. *Standard Edition*, 14:243–258. London: Hogarth Press, 1957.

—— (1919), Introduction to *Psycho-analysis and the war neuroses*. *Standard Edition*, 17:207–210. London: Hogarth Press, 1955.

—— (1920), Beyond the pleasure principle. *Standard Edition*, 18:7–64. London: Hogarth Press, 1955.

—— (1923), The ego and the id. *Standard Edition*, 19:12–66. London: Hogarth Press, 1961.

—— (1924a), The economic problem of masochism. *Standard Edition*, 19:159–170. London: Hogarth Press, 1961.

—— (1924b), The dissolution of the Oedipus complex. *Standard Edition*, 19:173–179. London: Hogarth Press, 1961.

—— (1926), Inhibitions, symptoms and anxiety. *Standard Edition*, 20:87–174. London: Hogarth Press, 1959.

—— (1930), Civilization and its discontents. *Standard Edition*, 21:64–145. London: Hogarth Press, 1961.

—— (1933), New introductory lectures on psycho-analysis. *Standard Edition*, 22:5–182. London: Hogarth Press, 1964.

—— (1937), Analysis terminable and interminable. *Standard Edition*, 23:216–253. London: Hogarth Press, 1964.

———— (1940), An outline of psycho-analysis. *Standard Edition*, 23:144–207. London: Hogarth Press, 1964.

Frosch, J. (1983), *The Psychotic Process*. New York: International Universities Press.

Gedo, J.E. (1980), Reflections on some current controversies in psychoanalysis. *J. Amer. Psychoanal. Assn.*, 28:331–362.

Gill, M.M. (1954), Psychoanalysis and exploratory psychotherapy. *J. Amer. Psychoanal. Assn.*, 2:771–797.

———— (1977), Psychic energy reconsidered: Discussion. *J. Amer. Psychoanal. Assn.*, 25:581–589.

———— (1979), The analysis of the transference. *J. Amer. Psychoanal. Assn.*, Supplement:263–288.

———— & Klein, G.S. (1967), *The Collected Papers of David Rapaport*. New York: Basic Books.

Glover, E. (1938), The psychoanalysis of affects. In: *On the Early Development of Mind: Selected Papers*. New York: International Universities Press, 1956, pp. 297–306.

———— (1947), *Basic Mental Concepts*. London: Imago.

———— (1955), *The Technique of Psychoanalysis*. New York: International Universities Press.

———— (1968), *The Birth of the Ego*. New York: International Universities Press.

Goldberg, A., ed. (1978), *The Psychology of the Self: A Casebook*. New York: International Universities Press.

Greenacre, P. (1968), The psychoanalytic process, transference, and acting out. *Internat. J. Psycho-Anal.*, 49:211–218.

Guntrip, H. (1961), *Personality Structure and Human Interaction*. New York: International Universities Press.

Hartmann, H. (1955), Notes on the theory of sublimation. *The Psychoanalytic Study of the Child*, 10:9–29. New York: International Universities Press.

———— & Loewenstein, R.M. (1962), Notes on the superego. *The Psychoanalytic Study of the Child*, 17:42–81. New York: International Universities Press.

Jacobson, E. (1953), The affects and their pleasure-unpleasure qualities in relation to the psychic discharge process. In: *Affects, Drives and Behavior*, vol. 1, ed. R.M. Loewenstein. New York: International Universities Press.

———— (1964), *The Self and the Object World*. New York: International Universities Press.

Jokl, R.H. (1950), Psychic determinism and preservation of sublimation in classical psychoanalytic procedure. *Bull. Menninger Clin.*, 14:207–219.

Jones, E. (1957), *The Life and Work of Sigmund Freud*, vol. 3. New York: Basic Books.

Klein, M. (1981), On Mahler's autistic and symbiotic phases. *Psychoanal. & Contemp. Thought*, 4:69–105.

Kohut, H. (1971), *The Analysis of the Self*. New York: International Universities Press.

———— & Wolf, E.S. (1978), The disorders of the self and their treatment: an outline. *Internal. J. Psycho-Anal.*, 59:413–425.

Kramer, S. (1977), Ethological contributions to the medical and behavioral sciences. In: *The Future of Animals, Cells, Models and Systems in Research, Development, Education and Testing*. Washington: National Academy of Science, pp. 76–114.

Kris, E. (1951), Ego psychology and interpretation in psychoanalytic therapy. *Psychoanal. Quart.*, 10:15–30.

———— (1952), *Psychoanalytic Explorations in Art*. New York: International Universities Press.

Laplanche, J., & Pontalis, J.-B. (1973), *The Language of Psychoanalysis*. New York: Norton.

Lewin, B. (1950), *The Psychoanalysis of Elation*. New York: Norton.

———— (1954), Sleep, narcissistic neurosis, and the analytic situation. *Psychoanal. Quart.*, 23:487–510.

———— (1955), Dream psychology and the analytic situation. *Psychoanal. Quart.*, 24:169–199.

Lewy, E. (1941), The return of the repression. *Bull Menninger Clin.*, 5:47–55.

———— (1961), Responsibility, free will and ego psychology. *Internat. J. Psycho-Anal.*, 42:260–270.

Lipton, S.L. (1977), The advantage of Freud's technique as shown in his analysis of the rat man. *Internat. J. Psycho-Anal.*, 58:255–274.

Loewald, H. (1960), On the therapeutic action of psycho-analysis. *Internat. J. Psycho-Anal.*, 41:16–33.

———— (1962), Internalization, separation, mourning, and the superego. *Psychoanal. Quart.*, 31:483–504.

———— (1973), On internalization. *Internat. J. Psycho-Anal.*, 54:9–18.

———— (1978), Primary process, secondary process, and language. In: *Psychoanalysis and Language, Psychiatry and the Humanities*, 3:235–270, ed. Joseph H. Smith. New Haven: Yale University Press.

Lorenz, K. (1955), On the killing of members of the same species. Uber das Töten von Artgenossen. Jahrb. d. Max-Planck-Ges. (1955), 105–140.

———— (1963), *On Aggression*. New York: Harcourt, Brace and World.

———— (1964), Ritualized fighting. In: *The Natural History of Aggression*, ed. J.D. Carthy & J.F. Ebling. New York: Academic Press, pp. 39–50.

———— (1965a), *Evolution and Modification of Behavior*. Chicago: University of Chicago Press.

—— (1965b), Preface to *The Expression of the Emotions in Man and Animals* by C. Darwin. Chicago: University of Chicago Press.

Lustman, S.L. (1969), Introduction to panel on the use of the economic viewpoint in clinical psychoanalysis. *Internat. J. Psycho-Anal.*, 50:95–102.

Macalpine, I. (1950), The development of the transference. *Psychoanal. Quart.*, 19:501–539.

Meissner, W.W. (1980), The problem of internalization and structure formation. *Internat. J. Psycho-Anal.*, 61:237–248.

Menninger, K. (1958), *Theory of Psychoanalytic Technique*. New York: Basic Books.

Novey, S. (1958), Mental representation of objects. *Psychoanal. Quart.*, 27:57–79.

Oppenheimer, R. (1956), Analogy in science. *American Psychologist*, 2:127–135.

Ornstein, P. (1974), On narcissism: Beyond the introduction: Highlights of Heinz Kohut's contributions to the psychoanalytic treatment of narcissistic personality disorders. *The Annual of Psychoanalysis*, 2:127–149, New York: International Universities Press.

Rangell, L. (1954), The psychology of poise. *Internat. J. Psycho-Anal.*, 35:313–332.

—— (1968a), A further attempt to solve the problem of anxiety. *J. Amer. Psychoanal. Assn.*, 16:371–404.

—— (1968b), A point of view on acting out. *Internat. J. Psycho-Anal.*, 49:195–201.

—— (1974), Toward a theory of affects: Panel reported by P. Castelnuovo-Tedesco. *J. Amer. Psychoanal. Assn.*, 22:612–625.

—— (1982), The self in psychoanalytic theory. *J. Amer. Psychoanal. Assn.*, 30:863–891.

Rapaport, D. (1960), *The Collected Papers of David Rapaport*, ed. M.M. Gill, New York: Basic Books.

—— & Gill, M.M. (1959), The points of view and assumptions of metapsychology. *Internat. J. Psycho-Anal.*, 40:153–162.

Reich, A. (1950), On the termination of analysis. *Internat. J. Psycho-Anal.*, 31:179–183.

Rosenblatt, A.D., & Thickstun, J.T. (1970), A study of the concept of psychic energy. *Internat. J. Psycho-Anal.*, 51:265–278.

—— —— (1977a), Energy, information and motivation: A revision of psychoanalytic theory. *J. Amer. Psychoanal. Assn.*, 25:537–588.

—— —— (1977b), Modern psychoanalytic concepts in a general psychology. *Psychological Issues*, 42/43. New York: International Universities Press.

Rothstein, A. (1980), Toward a critique of the psychology of the self. *Psychoanal. Quart.*, 49:423–455.

Sandler, J. (1976), Dreams, unconscious fantasies and identity of perception. *Internat. Rev. Psycho-Anal.*, 3:33–42.

—— & Rosenblatt, B. (1962), The concept of the representational world. *The Psychoanalytic Study of the Child*, 17:128–145. New York: International Universities Press.

Schafer, R. (1968), *Aspects of Internalization*. New York: International Universities Press.

—— (1976), *A New Language for Psychoanalysis*. New Haven: Yale University Press.

Schur, M. (1955), Comments on the metapsychology of somatization. *The Psychoanalytic Study of the Child*, 10:119–164. New York: International Universities Press.

—— (1966), *The Id and the Regulatory Principles of Mental Functioning*. New York: International Universities Press.

—— (1972), *Freud: Living and Dying*. New York: International Universities Press.

Segal, H. (1964), *Introduction to the Work of Melanie Klein*. New York: Basic Books.

Shaw, J.A. (1978), Man and the problem of aggression. *J. Phil. Assn. Psychoanal.*, 5:41–53.

Slap, J.W., ed. (1979), Interdisciplinary perspectives on psychoanalytic theories of aggression. *J. Amer. Psychoanal. Assn.*, 27:655–664.

Socarides, C.W. (1958), The function of moral masochism. *Internat. J. Psycho-Anal.*, 39:587–597.

Spiegel, L.A. (1978), Moral masochism. *Psychoanal. Quart.*, 47:209–236.

Stone, L. (1961), *The Psychoanalytic Situation*. New York: International Universities Press.

Wallace, L. (1963), The mechanism of shame. *Arch. Gen. Psychiat.*, 8:80–85.

—— (1969), Psychotherapy of a male homosexual. *Psychoanal. Rev.*, 56:346–364.

—— (1975), Observations on the psychoanalytic treatment of a patient with multiple sclerosis. *Internat. Rev. Psycho-Anal.*, 2:65–77.

Wallerstein, R.W. (1977), Psychic energy reconsidered: Introduction. *J. Amer. Psychoanal. Assn.*, 29:529–536.

Name Index

Alexander, F., 133
Anthony, E.J., 87
Arlow, J., 136

Benedek, T., 121
Beres, D., 66, 67, 86, 93
Berliner, B., 12-13
Blum, H.P., 51, 72
Bonaparte, Marie, 50
Brenner, C., 84, 87, 93

Darwin, C., 24, 25

Erikson, E.H., 121
Evans, R.I., 36

Fairbairn, W.R.D., 29
Fenichel, O., 64, 89, 94, 120, 121
Fleming, J., 122
Freud, Anna, 49
Freud, Sigmund, ix, x, xi, xiii, xiv, 3-14, 16, 17, 20, 23-28, 30, 33, 37, 39, 42-44, 46-50, 53, 54, 59-62, 64, 67, 68, 72, 73, 83, 86, 88-92, 94, 98, 100, 114, 119-121, 139-141, 143, 145, 146, 154, 162, 169
Frosch, J., 60

Gedo, J.E., 158
Gill, M.M., xi, 3, 4, 99, 142, 143
Glover, E., ix, 26, 60, 75, 81, 83, 84
Goldberg, A., 28, 158, 163, 165, 166
Greenacre, P., 100, 101, 116, 121, 157
Guntrip, H., 29

Hartmann, H., 3, 47, 49, 64, 65, 67

Jacobson, E., 69, 84
Jokl, R.H., 54
Jones, E., 50

Klein, M., 3, 28-29, 78
Kohut, H., 29, 98, 139, 158-169
Kramer, S., 24, 25
Kris, E., 119, 157

Laplanche, J., 60, 62, 63
Lewin, B., 98, 153, 156, 158, 162
Lewy, E., 27, 55
Lipton, S.L., 28, 119, 120, 121, 136
Loewald, H., xi, 51, 65, 66, 74, 76, 80, 124, 130
Loewenstein, R.M., 64, 65, 67
Lorenz, K., xii, 23, 24, 27, 33-38, 42, 51, 56
Lustman, S.L., 4

Macalpine, I., 121, 141, 142, 143, 144, 168
Meissner, W.W., 70, 71, 72
Menninger, K., 142, 144

Novey, S., 10

Oppenheimer, Robert, viii
Ornstein, P., 160

Pontalis, J.B., 60, 62, 63

Rangell, L., 72, 85, 86, 87, 114
Rapaport, D., xi, 53

185

Subject Index

Acting out, 114-115, 151, 152
Adaptive viewpoint, xi
Affects, 82-94
  anxiety, 86; *see also* Anxiety
  apathy, 93-94
  boredom, 94
  classification of, 83-84
  depression, 89-94; *see also*
    Depression
  definition of, 59
  envy, 88-89
  frustration, 85; *see also* Frustration
  instinctual elements in, 85-86
  multiple functions of, 85
  shame and guilt, 86-89, 93
  summary of, 94
  unified theory of, 84-85
Aggression, x, xii-xiii, 18, 23-42,
    175-178
  adaptiveness of, 33-36
  bond behavior and, 35-36
  clinical disparities with theory
    of, 27-33
  clinical example of, 31-33, 40-41
  discharge onto scapegoats of,
    39, 41
  displacement without neutralization of, 39-42
  displacement/discharge of, 38-41
  empathy as therapeutic modality and, 28
  ethological perspective on, xii-xiii, 23-25
  evidence for vs consciousness
    of, 31
  fantasies and, 29

Freud on, x, 23-33
Freud vs ethological view of, 24-27
Kohut on, 166-167
libidinal instincts and, *see* Libidinal and aggressive instincts
Lorenz on, 33-38
neurophysiological model of, 24-25
neurosis and, 38-42
ritualized displacement of, 34-37
sublimations of, 43-45
theoretical revisions that diminish role of, 28-31
working through, 31-33
Aggressive drive, concept of, 52
Ambivalent identifications, 129-130, 176
Ambivalent representations, 81, 82
Analogy in scientific research, viii
Analysis, *see* Psychoanalytic treatment
Analyst, gratification to, 170-171
Analyst's therapeutic stance
  empathic, 28, 161, 162
  neutrality, 99-100
  personal relationship, 120
  silence, 28, 135-139, 150, 158
Anger, Kohut's approach to, 166-167
Anxiety, 86, 94
  Kohut on, 167-168
  psysiological accompaniments of,
    5-6
  redefined, 5

187